EVANGELISM
REMIXED

EMPOWERING STUDENTS FOR
COURAGEOUS AND CONTAGIOUS FAITH

DAVE RAHN & TERRY LINHART

ZONDERVAN®

ZONDERVAN.com/
AUTHORTRACKER
follow your favorite authors

youth
specialties

YOUTH SPECIALTIES

Evangelism Remixed: Empowering Students for Courageous and Contagious Faith
Copyright 2009 by Dave Rahn and Terry Linhart

Youth Specialties resources, 300 S. Pierce St., El Cajon, CA 92020 are published by Zondervan, 5300 Patterson Ave. SE, Grand Rapids, MI 49530.

Library of Congress Cataloging-in-Publication Data

Rahn, Dave, 1954-
  Evangelism remixed : empowering students for courageous and contagious
faith / Dave Rahn and Terry Linhart.
      p. cm.
  Includes bibliographical references (p.   ).
  ISBN 978-0-310-29293-7 (soft cover)
  1. Evangelistic work—Study and teaching. 2. Christian education of
young people. 3. Church work with youth. I. Linhart, Terry, 1964- II.
Title.
  BV3796.R35 2009
  269'.20712—dc22   2008049948

All Scripture quotations, unless otherwise indicated, are taken from the *Holy Bible, Today's New International Version™*. TNIV®. Copyright 2001, 2005 by International Bible Society. Used by permission of Zondervan. All rights reserved.

Any Internet addresses (websites, blogs, etc.) and telephone numbers printed in this book are offered as a resource. They are not intended in any way to be or imply an endorsement by Youth Specialties, nor does Youth Specialties vouch for the content of these sites and numbers for the life of this book.

Cover and interior design by Mark Novelli

Printed in the United States of America

09 10 11 12 13 14 • 20 19 18 17 16 15 14 13 12 11 10 9 8 7 6 5 4 3 2 1

DEDICATION

To Susie and Kelly:

We know that it's not been easy living with us
"change-the-world" types and are forever grateful
to God for the grace he has given you—and you give
us—as we've journeyed together.

ACKNOWLEDGMENTS

Thanks to Jay Howver and Roni Meek for guiding us through this project. We are deeply indebted to Jeremy Jones for his editing and coaching expertise—and to David, Jen, Welch, Erin, Michaela, Heather, and Mark for making the book look good and read well.

A majority of the research for this book was conducted with student teams from Huntington University. We want to extend special appreciation to the trio of Ben Hamm, Christy Cabe, and Dave Ramseyer for giving particular shape to our project. Thanks also to the 22 youth workers and 424 students who participated in the study.

Finally, we'd like to express great fondness and appreciation for each other. But we don't know how to do that without getting too weird. Suffice it to say that the journey for years as colleagues has been deep and wonderfully enriching, a bonus gift from God to lives that are already full of joy and wonder.

CONTENTS

Introduction   09

Chapter One: Heart-Shaping   12

Chapter Two: Adults as Mentors   27

Chapter Three: Ready or Not   48

Chapter Four: Adults as Program Providers   66

Chapter Five: Program Focus—Praying Hard   86

Chapter Six: Program Focus—Inviting Often   98

Chapter Seven: Program Focus—Explaining Well   115

Chapter Eight: Tracking the Change   130

Appendix: Research Tools   145

Endnotes   164

INTRODUCTION

When I was a high school senior, Hank Altorfer of Young Life whispered in my (Dave's) ear that he thought I had what it takes to be a Young Life leader. T.A. Strader of Youth for Christ (YFC) had already challenged me to be sure that my year's priorities were aligned with the Lord's. Pastor Roger Birdsall drilled a rock-solid confidence in God's Word into the fabric of my young soul; his sons Doug and Brent showed me how following Jesus could be a great adventure. Another Young Life leader, Marv Kelso, organized us into the most intense peer discipleship groups I've ever seen. My friend Dick Mergener taught me to pray with my eyes open while driving. Jeff Carroll, another friend, teamed up with me to start and lead our own weekly Bible study. And after my friend Denny Huebner came to Christ as a result of our endless conversations next to the swimming pool, he took over the leadership of this Bible study outreach.

Back in 1971 and 1972 when all of this was happening, no one was talking about student leadership in youth ministry. In fact, there weren't a lot of people doing youth ministry!

But nothing rings as true as your own experience. So for years I have been convinced and taught that young people can do amazing things to reach their friends for Christ and help them grow in Christ. I've never believed they do this on their own, or that it was preferable for them to attempt to do so. Adults can be life-changing assets when they're clear-minded about how they can invest in the teens with whom they connect.

The idea for this book came out of a research project Terry did while obtaining his master's degree at Huntington University. It so happened that this was the program I led, and we shared a passion to find out what we could about student leaders who are defined especially by their effective influence on their non-Christian friends. As we drilled down into the nitty-gritty of research, we identified two questions to guide this study:

1) *What are the differences between student leaders who reach their friends for Christ and those who don't?*

2) *What are the common factors in youth ministries where teens reaching teens for Christ is the norm?*

For two years Terry and I, along with 10 trained students from Huntington University's undergrad youth ministry program, traveled in teams across the country conducting on-site visits, interviews, discussions, observations, and survey collections from 22 different groups. We found these groups by following up via phone on the 109 different nominations' youth ministries in which it was a common and historical practice for teens to reach friends for Christ. (We've included some of the instruments we used in the Appendix if you want to check them out.) When the dust settled on our travel (funded through the generosity of the MacLeod Foundation), 424 student leaders and their adult youth ministry leaders had participated in this research. Sophisticated data analysis—including one-way analyses of variances (ANOVAs) to determine differences between student groupings, and lots of pouring over the qualitative information collected—led to the robust and significant findings presented in this book. Groups from Texas (5), California (4), Illinois (3), Indiana (2), Washington (2), Colorado (1), Kansas (1), Michigan (1), Ohio (1), Pennsylvania (1), and Massachusetts (1) participated in this study, giving us confidence that we've made a reliable contribution to the body of knowledge that exists on the subjects of student leadership and youth evangelism—even though our design does not allow us to claim a true *national* sampling.

In the 10 years since we completed this project, we each have had the opportunity to engage in additional research. Where any of it touches on the findings of the original project we have included such insights in this book's discussions. Endnotes will help interested readers track down that additional information in greater detail.

We have also been pretty actively engaged in testing our findings through real-life ministry experiences. Groups such as the national Fellowship of Christian Athletes and Youthfront in Kansas City have adjusted some of their strategies over the years based upon our contributions.

In all honesty, that's why we're writing. We think the Lord has given us something that may be helpful to brothers and sisters who dream of unleashing the potential of their best young people for leadership impact. There are lots of Christian adults like Hank, T.A., Roger, and Marv (named earlier) who want to invest in young people. They hope to maximize teens' development as followers of Christ, believing they can become contributors to the mission of God and, ultimately, influential friends among their peers. We share their passion and pray this book is useful in their journey.

CHAPTER ONE
HEART-SHAPING

Do any of the following sound like stories from your experience?

Rich is leaving his current ministry. He's been effective in the task he was asked to do, but a few months ago frustration and anger gained the upper hand in his life. Underpaid, underappreciated, and overburdened, this young man desperately needed someone to help him see his life in larger perspective. Instead he stumbles on largely alone, serving his church 70 to 80 hours a week, exhausted by a cause that once invigorated him.

Consider the case of Jill, a popular high school student especially valued for her ability to attract other kids to youth meetings. As a student leader she is hugely appreciated by her zealous youth director, but he doesn't know that she desperately wishes she could find the courage to talk with someone about her sexual-identity struggles.

Fred is a talented, all-star student athlete who has so much to offer his youth group that adult leaders ask a great deal of him—without regard for how the long hours and scattered focus impact Fred's ability to be a faithful family member, friend, student, or athlete.

The local student ministry is never so energized as when Julie is involved. She throws herself into every meeting with contagious enthusiasm, drawing praise from her youth pastor for her contributions to the kingdom. There is just one problem: When Julie attempts to share Christ with her non-Christian classmates, she's worse than a telemarketer—always in sales mode, communicating a picture of God's kingdom that is both unattractive and inaccurate.

There's a lot at stake here. In our performance-oriented culture, larger kingdom values can get lost in finger-pointing and shoulder-shrugging as ministers assigned to specialized roles on multi-staff teams concentrate on doing their own tasks with excellence. Whose responsibility is it to protect each person's wholeness and spiritual health? How can it be okay for us to ask more and more of students without regard for how we might be further fragmenting their lives?

Are student ministries part of the solution, or part of the problem?

Proverbs 4:23 says, "Above all else, guard your heart, for it is the wellspring of life" (NIV). Who will show today's students how to put this priority into practice, if not those of us who lead youth ministries?

Involving harried kids in our particular ministries may be important, but it is no guarantee that it will result in God-honoring fruit. We sometimes act like our youth ministry niche absolves us from reckoning with a person's all-of-life responsibilities before God. Examples of this folly jump off the pages of newspapers with alarming frequency, reminding us of the consequences of such neglect. Years ago O.J. Simpson attained his celebrity icon status, not because of his entire life, but because of limited, specialized accomplishments on the football field (and, to a lesser degree, in movies). Now his name is infamous for other reasons. Baseball records may be marked with asterisks because overachieving stars used illegal steroids to cheat. Politicians on both sides of the aisle insist their job performance is all that matters, and by reelecting them the American people largely agree.

We live in a culture saturated by advertisements. Malls are as much recreational sites as locations for making necessary purchases. Routine upgrades for computers and cell phones are a way of life. These collective forces combine with our hurried pace of life to drive wedges into our hearts, effectively partitioning our lives so that integrated thinking doesn't disrupt our decision-making processes. It's troubling that our ministry culture is so similar. Who expresses competent care for our wholeness?

We need to break this cycle in our work with students. And if we're not even clear about how to form *the most responsive* of our young people for a life of joyful service and obedience to our Lord Jesus, you can bet we'll stumble with everyone else who has been entrusted to our care.

THE HEART IS OUR TARGET

These observations might seem like a strange lead-in to a book about helping students step up to their fullest potential of world impact. Our goal is to champion *leadership-as-influence* for young people. Students who are effective in this largely informal kind of leadership will be marked by a courageous and contagious faith, attributes that ensure a timeless connection to the mission of God in the world. *That*, as they say, *will preach.*

The disconnect between a missional focus and our earlier whole-person plea is because so many of us view outreach as an add-on to an already overscheduled life. If evangelism is seen as one more thing to do, it only contributes to the burdensome pile-on that so many of us experience in ministry. We totally agree. The convoluted and complex way we're trying to patch together our Christ-following obligations today can't be God's plan for us, can it?

So let's all stop, take a deep breath, and huddle to get on the same page. We believe that the heart of each individual young person needs to become the agreed-upon target for everything we do in youth ministry. Well guarded and properly formed, this heart is the source out of which Jesus' supernatural power transforms our character and impacts our culture. The heart is the key to *becoming* different and then *making* a difference. So grab a cup of coffee and take a reflective stroll through the following samples from Scripture—the emphases are ours. See if you don't agree that when it comes to God's ministry focus, the *heart* is where the action is:

"Love the LORD your God with *all your heart* and with all your soul and with all your strength." (Deuteronomy 6:5)

"But be very careful to keep the commandment and the law that Moses the servant of the LORD gave you: to love the LORD your God, to walk in obedience to him, to keep his commands, to hold fast to him and *to serve him with all your heart* and with all your soul." (Joshua 22:5)

"Trust in him at all times, you people; *pour out your hearts* to him, for God is our refuge…. Do not trust in extortion or put vain hope in stolen goods; though your riches increase, *do not set your heart* on them." (Psalms 62:8,10)

"Trust in the LORD with *all your heart* and lean not on your own understanding; in all your ways submit to him, and he will make your paths straight." (Proverbs 3:5-6)

"This is what the LORD says: 'Cursed are those who trust in mortals, who depend on flesh for their strength and whose hearts turn away from the LORD.'" (Jeremiah 17:5)

"Good people bring good things out of the good *stored up in their heart,* and evil people bring evil things out of the evil *stored up in their heart.* For out of the *overflow of the heart* the mouth speaks." (Luke 6:45)

"*Do not let your hearts be troubled.* Trust in God; trust also in me." (John 14:1)

"If you declare with your mouth, 'Jesus is Lord,' and believe in your heart that God raised him from the dead, you will be saved." (Romans 10:9)

"Therefore judge nothing before the appointed time; wait till the Lord comes. He will bring to light what is hidden in darkness and will expose the motives of people's hearts. At that time each will receive theirs praise from God." (1 Corinthians 4:5)

"I pray that out of his glorious riches he may strengthen you with power through his Spirit in your inner being, so that Christ may dwell in your hearts through faith. And I pray that you, being rooted and established in love, may have power, together with all the Lord's people, to grasp how wide and long and high and deep is the love of Christ, and to know this love that surpasses knowledge—that you may be filled to the measure of all the fullness of God." (Ephesians 3:16-19)

"May he *strengthen your hearts* so that you will be blameless and holy in the presence of our God and Father when our Lord Jesus comes with all his holy ones." (1 Thessalonians 3:13)

"But *in your hearts* revere Christ as Lord. Always be prepared to give an answer to everyone who asks you to give the reason for the hope that you have. But do this with gentleness and respect." (1 Peter 3:15)

For more examples, check out Deuteronomy 13:3, Deuteronomy 30:6, 1 Kings 11:2, Psalms 28:7, Psalms 33:21, Psalms 112:7, Proverbs 3:3, John 5:42, Acts 1:24, Acts 11:23, Acts 16:14, Romans 15:6 (NIV), Ephesians 1:17-19, Colossians 2:1-3, Colossians 3:22-23, and 2 Thessalonians 3:4-5.

HEARTS FORMED FOR GOD

By targeting the heart we will be person-centered in our ministry with—and to—students. We think we need to make it a priority to strengthen their hearts, helping young people acquire the virtue of courage. Students who are courageous will willingly face challenges and take risks. They are confident in the constant presence of a loving God, unafraid to take unpopular stands where an exceptional character reveals them to be different from their peers. We don't want to minimize the fact that in the social economy of teenagers choosing to align with the Lord when no one else wants to do so takes strength of character. God is always on a mission, constantly working out his grand rescue plan (see Ephesians 1:9-10 and Colossians 1:15-20). The participation he requires of his people includes identifying with him courageously.

As Joshua prepared to assume leadership from Moses, he heard at least seven different times a message we want to bury as a treasure deep in the hearts of our young people: Be strong and courageous (Deuteronomy 31:6, 7, 23 and Joshua 1:6, 7, 9, 18). David passed this same advice to his son, Solomon, urging the world's most famous Wise Guy to finish the work of the temple because the Lord would be with him and not let him down (read it in 1 Chronicles 28:20).

Teens face their own daunting challenges today, and their hearts are every bit as vulnerable as those of their biblical ancestors. Like Joshua and Solomon, young people fortify their hearts by acquiring a mature understanding of the trustworthiness of the Lord Jesus Christ.

Herein lies a clue for all of us interested in seeing students become courageous Christians. What will it take for young people to know that the Lord is with them always and that his indwelling presence makes all the difference in every circumstance? How can we help them live openly and authentically as Jesus-followers in touch with the reality of the Holy Spirit within? What can we do so teens will see how their personal stories are—in fact—embedded in the grand, dynamic story of God? Though we seek these mission-essential outcomes for our students, we dare not approach this agenda as some extra-credit opportunity for the select few who are wired for outreach. Rather, we lock onto our heart-shaping focus, determined to bring about biblical maturity as the faith soil that produces all kinds of wondrous fruit—including the courage required to participate in the mission of God.

MATURITY GROWS A COURAGEOUS FAITH

In the parable of the sower (Luke 8:1-15), the seed that is choked out by thorns—life's worries, riches, and pleasures—doesn't have a chance to reach the maturity for which it was intended. Paul could speak a message of wisdom among those who were mature (1 Corinthians 2:6). He felt that those who were mature would be able to understand the clear priority of knowing and gaining Christ that would, by comparison, make any other pursuit feel like wallowing in the dung pile (Philippians 3). The apostle also gave maturity an endpoint status in his description of the pattern of ministry (Ephesians 4:13). He further identified maturity as the goal of Epaphras' prayer for the Colossians, that they "may stand firm in all the will of God, mature and fully assured" (Colossians 4:12b). The writer of Hebrews uses the word *maturity* as a practical benchmark to distinguish persons who may still be learning the elementary teachings about Christ from those who are ready for a more solid spiritual diet (Hebrews 6:1). Those who are mature attained such status as a result of continuously practicing their understanding of the rule of Jesus in their lives (Hebrews 5:14). James links maturity to our ability to hang in there as learners until the toughest teacher of all—life's difficult experiences—can bring about our character transformation (James 1).

This picture of maturity in Scripture sketches persons who are deeply rooted in biblical truth—so deeply that Jesus Christ operates as the unchallenged, unshakeable Lord of their lives. Knowing him, as Joshua did, is the source of courageous living. *When our students' faith becomes mature, they will know Jesus Christ truly and personally, submitting to his lordship in their lives and consequently receiving the benefit of courageous hearts.*

Because Jesus really exists, students can either be accurate or off base in their knowledge of him. They need to know him *truly*, a standard too many ignore.

Charles cruised through his youth group years satisfied with the level of common knowledge he could pick up from the weekly lessons. His interest in the worship band held his attention for a while, and his skills as a guitar player made him in demand for a traveling ministry group. But living without clear convictions rooted in biblical truth, he eventually wandered into some of the temptations that come from being in the spotlight all the time. Charles had been socialized into the faith without acquiring knowledge of Jesus that was rooted in truth, clearly revealing what the Lord expects from those who follow him.

Because Jesus really cares, students can build a relationship with him as they walk through all of life with him. They need to know him *personally*, a goal for which too many pay only lip service.

Debi was a Bible Quiz champ, and everyone had high expectations for her as she headed off to the Christian college of her choice. A month later she was kicked out for breaking all sorts of lifestyle agreements, going into a faith tailspin from which she couldn't recover. Her story illustrates the reality that knowing biblical factoids is no guarantee of a mature faith in the living Lord—a truth that any open-minded Pharisee might have learned from Jesus himself back in the day.

Some in our postmodern culture invite us to consider *only* the Jesus of our own experience, claiming that our personal encounter is all the truth we need. At the other extreme are those who can clinically dissect the historical record of Jesus' life, but cannot identify a reservoir of life-changing experiences that testify to the reality that Jesus Christ has been, and still is, active in their personal transformation. Both of these approaches are inadequate. A mature faith will open the pipeline and allow biblical truth to circulate in our lives, truth that encompasses a body of knowledge to be learned and a personal reality to be experienced.

Let's say we want to equip our students for peer evangelism. We may sign them up for some formal classes and require some significant reading. There are those who, because of their diligent studies, will easily learn the content required in this course. If there were tests, those students would excel, and they'd be sitting pretty if grades were given for only their cognitive understanding of the material.

But while these goals may be adequate for an academic class, they're not sufficient for the journey of faith on which we need to launch our young people. We want them to experience the sweaty-palm nervousness that comes right before engaging someone in a spiritual conversation for the first time. We want them to hear their own tremendous capacity for making excuses for their evangelistic *inactivity*—excuses so reasonable and loud they make the Holy Spirit's voice tough to pick up. We want them to encounter the diverse interest levels of their friends. Some are hungry for the gospel; others are clearly apathetic to all things spiritual. Yet they're equally needy, and we want our students to grasp this important truth. Somehow, if they're really going to learn to reach their friends, they must experience the related realities of evangelism.

The same is true for all of us in the Christian faith. Jesus Christ didn't come only to be a teacher of precepts, but also to be a giver of life. We ought to teach young people the great, sweeping content of scriptural truth. We ought to help them study the details of biblical instruction. God's story needs to be known. But we also must coach them to practice the realities of God's Word in the daily routines of their lives. Those who are truly mature have an understanding of both elements located smack dab in the middle of their hearts, where courage grows strong or shrivels for lack of sustenance.

What if a student is effectively reaching his or her friends, but knows only the five verses that are contained in a favorite evangelistic tract? We hope you'll agree that the need for biblical maturity in such a teen's life is strong. We must never let short-term evangelistic successes keep us from focusing on shaping our hearts for long-term courageous faith. That focus also includes *faithfulness*.

FAITHFULNESS GROWS
A CONTAGIOUS FAITH

Understanding maturity is crucial to understanding how faith-fulness is a distinct concept, worthy of its own heart-shaping focus in our student ministries. Maturity seems to carry with it a sense of arrival or attainment. While it ought not to be confused with the ultimate end of perfection, it's a critical benchmark in our becoming like Jesus.

Faithfulness, on the other hand, relates exclusively to our *obedience* to God. Each opportunity in life presents a new opportunity to be faithful. As such, the context of any specific situation—including a person's gifts, abilities, experiences, insights, and God's personal directives—is critical to under-standing whether or not someone was faithful. The Bible in-dicates that faithfulness in smaller matters is a prerequisite for greater opportunities (Luke 19:11-26). Patterns of faith-fulness are likely more up and down than those of maturity. None of our students are at a faithfulness disadvantage due to their age. Nor are they—or we—excused from its relentless demands. Thank God for his grace and forgiveness!

How do we get a handle on faithfulness? It may be help-ful to consider how evaluating a student's faithfulness would differ from assessing his or her maturity. Think of maturity as the sort of standard children are judged by if they're allowed to go on the wilder rides at an amusement park. "You must be this tall," the sign says. Once someone attains the required height, they're tall enough to grab the thrill. Similarly, once a young person has developed a sufficient level of understand-ing about God and his expectations for us, he may be said to be mature.

By contrast, faithfulness is constantly open to measure-ment, married as it is to the moments of life. For example, any one of us who has had an impeccable record of faithful-ness over a two-year period may, in a weak moment, find that we have missed the mark and stand in need of repentance.

As such, faithfulness is probably best assessed by considering one's consistency of living. This isn't unlike how a basketball player judges free throw effectiveness. (The percentage of baskets made in relation to the opportunities to go to the line describes one's consistency.)

Every arena of life is fair game for raising questions about our level of faithfulness. Our students' character development, relationships, and vocational responsibilities are all connected to their faithfulness. Made to be moral beings, we will all be faithful by becoming the holy persons of integrity that Jesus wants us to be. Created for social connectivity, we will all measure up to faithfulness standards when we relate to others exactly how Jesus would want us to relate to them. Designed by God to take on responsibilities and assignments in the Kingdom, we want to be so in tune with the Lord that we can discern exactly what service he requires of us, and then have the courage to do just exactly what he wants. (These three major purposes for humanity can be seen in Genesis 2:15-18.)

When our students—or we—begin to acquire consistency in each faithfulness arena, our faith will take on a contagious nature. Matching a life that is attractive, selfless, hopeful, and substantive with loving, well-delivered, and timely words is the normal pattern of influence God expects from his people. Jesus himself promises to show us the way to live contagiously as full participants in the mission of God, offering to simplify the complexity of life's demands by teaching us the elegant rest that comes from focusing on faithfulness (Matthew 11:25-30).

Every life opportunity presents itself as a chance to be faithful again to the Lord...or not. Like the earlier mentioned basketball player, our progress will be evidenced as we become more consistent. To further illustrate, someone who regularly makes just five out of 10 basket attempts would love to increase the percentage of shots that are converted. If we respond faithfully in only five out of every 10 life chances, our clear goal becomes one of increasing our consistency in faithfulness. We can celebrate six out of 10 while setting our eyes on perfection. Presumably this is what it means to be "more faithful."

Faithfulness is identified as one of the more important matters of the law—something that was hypocritically neglected by some religious leaders (Matthew 23:23). Other parables point to the responsibility that one who is faithful assumes, and the fact that faithfully discharging the assigned responsibility ought to earn opportunities for even greater responsibilities (Matthew 24:45; 25:21-23). Many of the references to faithfulness in the New Testament are descriptors of particular persons. Thus, the term is defined in the examples of Timothy (1 Corinthians 4:17), the Ephesians (Ephesians 1:1), Epaphras (Colossians 1:7), Onesimus (Colossians 4:9), the Colossians (Colossians 1:2), Tychicus (Ephesians 6:21, Colossians 4:7), Moses (Hebrews 3:2, 5-6), Silas (1 Peter 5:12), and Gaius (3 John 3, 5). *Faithful* is an important descriptor used by John in his futuristic vision of the saints of God (Revelation 2:10, 13; 13:10; 14:12; 17:14), besides being the name of the Lord Jesus as White-Horse Rider (Revelation 19:11).

We are admonished by Paul to be faithful in prayer (Romans 12:12), prove our faithfulness after we've been given a trust (1 Corinthians 4:2), and walk in the Spirit in such a way that faithfulness is an evident fruit (Galatians 5:21-22). Paul's amazement at his being chosen by God for service may only be surpassed by his thankfulness for being considered faithful (1 Timothy 1:12).

No doubt Paul's jaw-dropping awe is due in part to his appreciation of the perfect faithfulness of the Lord Jesus in relation to us (1 Thessalonians 5:24; 2 Timothy 2:13; Hebrews 2:17). This is a great example of how maturity and faithfulness relate to each other. Our understanding of the Lord Jesus actually filters anything we hear from him. When we know him to be perfectly faithful to accomplish in us what he calls us to do, when we're certain that his call to us comes from his great love for us and others, then our own faithfulness resolve is strengthened. We experience not only a clear sense of direction from the Lord regarding our character, relationships, and tasks, but also the active empowering efforts of the Holy Spirit related to our motivation and perseverance.

We get *courageous.*

Our faith gets *contagious.*

LET'S FOLLOW THE PLAN

Can you see why an uncritical adoption of student ministry programs for leadership formation is insufficient to meet this depth of need? Person-centeredness—with its heart-shaping focus—gives us a chance.

Some who want to equip their students for evangelistic impact load most of their efforts into skill-developing programs. Such a strategy will likely see short-term outcomes that are not sustained over time. Isn't this the state of concern for youth ministry today? Haven't we seen a troubling faith fallout among too many students with whom we've ministered once they move into their college years and beyond? Though some of the research decrying this slide is dubious, our collective experiences confirm our worst fears.

It's time for a change.

Living as we do—between Eden and the new heaven and new Earth—we think our first priority should be to adjust to, rather than ignore, God's master design for persons. Those in the process of heart-shaping today's students can benefit from a tutorial reminder that we were blueprinted in the first garden to be continually responsive to God.

It doesn't matter whether we want to raise up students who serve on short-term mission teams, lead worship, reach their friends for Christ, love more authentically, or relate to their parents honorably. Whatever the desired outcome of our work with students, the ultimate source of success is the Holy Spirit's activity in their hearts.

By helping young people mature in their faith, we strengthen their heart's capacity for the natural challenges and risks of life. They live *courageously* for Jesus, anywhere and anytime.

Students face a vast array of opportunities, relationships, and obligations, as we all do. By coaching them to become more consistently faithful in how they respond to the situations they face, we help them train their hearts for a lifetime of following Jesus *contagiously*, bringing others along with them in the journey.

In this book we will focus on one part of our adventure. Based on original research and a boatload of personal experiences, we will offer insights to Christian adults who want to see the teens with whom they minister become students who reach their friends for Christ and help them grow in Christ. We acknowledge there is much more to this journey of faithfulness than to be evangelistically fruitful. But we would like to offer the reminder that evangelism is part of the faithfulness mix.

If we resist the temptation to become fidgety with particularistic program approaches to ministry, then the holistic design of God applied to student ministry will result in young people whose faith is courageous and contagious. Further, it's our conviction that *mission*—understood in both its broadest and most personal contexts—is what God is all about in this world. We hope these pages help us all get on board and, by God's grace, lead with the courage needed for our own faith to become *strategically* and *naturally* contagious. That's what the focus of the next chapter is all about.

CHAPTER TWO
ADULTS AS MENTORS

Wouldn't it be great if research, Scripture, or common sense provided a never-miss ministry checklist that guaranteed students would grow into leaders? What if there were a formula to produce teens who never compromised their personal integrity and who exercised natural, Christ-inspiring influence among their friends?

Beware of any promise to provide such a book of secrets; it doesn't exist. But adults *can* minister with more clarity than is commonly practiced. In fact, if adults don't cultivate and practice the sort of heart-shaping ministry expertise described in the last chapter, there's a high likelihood that students will never grab hold of this life-giving priority. And without it, their leadership development is sure to be retarded.

Like little league baseball coaches trying to introduce the fine art of hitting to their team, adults in student ministry must understand the complementary roles of vision and focus. To get a vision, or feel, of what a good hit is like, the coach might use a batting tee or pitch a bucket of balls to each player. Kids need to be able to picture the ball jumping off the bat as solid contact is made. They need to be convinced that a frozen-rope line drive is better than a fly ball. In fact, the counterproductive vision of a home run sailing over the fence can lead to a swing that results in too many pop-ups or strikeouts. When the vision is locked in, coaches find much greater fruitfulness as they talk about the elements of focus while hitting.

"Don't just see the ball when it comes in; see a spot on the ball."

"Hit the ball when it gets right in front of the plate."

"Watch the ball actually hit the bat; keep your head down all the way."

Plenty of baseball examples illustrate this truth: The truest work of a coach is to instill in players the fun and thrill of the game (vision) and connect it to persistent, skill-growing practice routines (focus). Similarly, the effort required to tighten our heart-shaping focus with students must be sustained by the compelling vision of teens who live large, authentic, and Christ-revealing lives among their friends.

And if our focus is not quite right, what then? Well, folks with a focus problem struggle in managing their efforts and time. At week's end they often feel drained from their activity, but bewildered by how relatively little they accomplished. Urgent stuff crowds out what's most important. It's not that what we do is done poorly; in fact it might be done very well. That may explain why it's difficult for those who don't focus well to consider whether what they spend their time doing should even be done at all.

So, possessed by the vision of helping students expand their lives in Christ to experience personal and relational fruitfulness, focus-impaired adults just don't do a good job with the daily details and processes of ministry necessary to shape a heart. What is important is clear to them; what to do next in order to accomplish what is important is the mystery.

Developing students for influence requires us to concentrate our efforts like a laser beam. The target? As discussed in the last chapter: *The hearts and lives of real teens, busily moving through a world that is hostile to the way of Jesus.* Point the laser in the wrong way and we won't succeed. Diffuse the light and we'll shed some light, but fail to burn a lasting imprint into students' hearts.

Some readers can't wait to hear about the program that will pull all of this together in the most practical way. Such ministry-as-program thinking may be the greatest obstacle to being truly person-centered in our focus.

A pastor friend once likened his work to that of employees who hustle around the local pizza buffet making sure there are plenty of different pizzas and a well-stocked salad bar. He saw ministry as providing opportunities for persons to come to Christ, grow in Christ, or be helped to serve Christ. A perfect illustration of a program-centered focus, the guardians of the buffet simply concentrate on what they provide. They conclude their customers are satisfied because the food disappears and people keep coming.

Persons do get fed this way. But there really is no guarantee you'll get the taco pizza you had a hankering for if a waiter never shows up at your table to ask you what you want. You'll eventually go elsewhere if you don't receive the focus of attention.

Some of us monitor attendance patterns and infer that students are growing into maturity and faithfulness. Others try to maintain program balance as a measure of ministry health. It's not that we can't use programs to develop student leaders; in fact, we'll likely need to use some effective programs to reach our goals. But our conviction is that we are less likely to misstep when we focus on developing *persons* rather than *programs*. Adults who see themselves as mentors are more likely to focus on their students. Driven by the vision of helping young people they love become more like Jesus, these adults are prepared to imitate Paul and do whatever it takes to make it happen (Colossians 1:28-29).

What *does* it take? Research sheds some light on timeless biblical principles and calls us to become purposefully flexible. Loving others amidst a culture swirling with change requires us to constantly make adjustments in our relationships for the sake of others. We see relational and purposeful flexibility at the heart of what it means to be a mentor. We've identified four focal points that can supply purposeful riverbanks through which we can channel the flow of life to students. They can provide us with a channel as we do whatever it takes to ensure that they grow into courageous followers of Christ, contagious in the way they influence their friends for Christ.

FLEX FOCUS 1: *ACT NATURALLY*

It's true: Adults must posses a clear picture of what a fruitful student leader looks like if they're going to be of any help. Begin with the end in mind, *yada yada*. But there is a fruit-bearing insight from Scripture that requires us to shift our attention from desired outcomes in students' lives. Don't pursue results that can only be delivered by God. Instead, understand *how* the Lord uses us to bring about his vision in a student's life and then focus *only* on doing our part in the process. We'll find more power by living within our assignment from God than in master-planning everyone's roles.

Jesus taught this in a number of ways, but his parable of a farmer scattering seed in Mark 4:26-29 may illustrate it best. He makes it clear that, though we may work hard, growth is a mysterious gift of God. We can cooperate with and enjoy this gift, but it's never under our control. We sow, God grows. Maybe we should call this a ministry relaxation technique, because we really do get to rest when we quit trying to control what we were never meant to control. Better yet, let's remember that this is how abiding in Christ is supposed to work (John 15).

It's a natural outcome of our connection to Christ that we be identified as followers of Jesus and draw individuals within our sphere of influence into this journey with us. Courageous and contagious students emerge out of such a faithful process in God's time and because of the work of the Holy Spirit. Dann Spader, founder of Sonlife Ministries, famously likened this process to the explosive transformation of popcorn kernels into popcorn. We only wish the transformation of our students was as instantaneous and predictable.

This much we know: The biblical change process differs significantly from management-informed approaches to recruiting and screening students for leadership. Youth pastors employing an organizational way of thinking might send out a wide invitation to would-be student leaders, collect responses on lengthy application forms, check references, and conduct probing interviews. Even when that process is done thoroughly, it can't possibly compete with what we learn about students when we connect with them through biblical disciple-making relationships.

We need to be led into a form of student leadership that more faithfully translates Jesus' pattern with his disciples into our 21st century context. To unpack this and better understand our role in the process, let's dig into the Lord's original mandate for making disciples.

The sole command in the Great Commission (Matthew 28:18-20) is to *make* disciples. *Going, baptizing, and teaching them to obey* are used to modify that command. We leverage our impact when we shift our focus from the resulting outcome to these three subtasks. These are roles we can handle. God brings about the real change in someone's life. John's version of the Great Commission (John 20:21) supplies a key clue to discovering how all this should look in our lives. We can pick up style points by going about disciple-making in the same natural way Jesus did. Unpacking these three modifiers is a great way to understand—and copy—Jesus' approach.

We quickly move to the conclusion that this assignment is not just for specialists, but for everyone who follows Christ.

So whatever we do as adults has to be transferable to students. They, too, get to be used by God to help make disciples. Locating the natural power within the concepts of going, baptizing, and teaching to obey will reveal the benefit of releasing student leaders for courageous and contagious living.

Most translations of the Great Commission imply that we are commanded to go to other locations—like missionaries—in order to make disciples. This might have been true if the participle *going* (perhaps more accurately understood as "while going") were actually the imperative *go*. We don't mean to say it's not important to travel to exotic places to serve the Lord, if that's where we're called. But Matthew's passage simply doesn't teach that. Instead it affirms that God will use us to make disciples while we're cruising through life.

Naturally moving among non-Christians enables us to be contagious carriers of the faith. "While going" is as natural as it gets. For example, when Joel wanted to reach others for Christ, it only made sense for him to start a Bible study with his basketball teammates. That's where he lived and put most of his energy. In the same way students can develop real, transformational relationships with others as a part of the normal ebb and flow of their lives. Isn't it clear that they will have at least some advantages over adults when it comes to teen ministry? Youth culture is where a student's natural life journey takes place. When we adults want to hang out in Teenville, we need to be deliberate and even courageous, crossing bridges from our world to theirs. This is not to say that there aren't good reasons for adults to take such journeys. But we'll never be as naturally connected to teens as other young people can be.

"Baptizing" points to another focus as God grows disciples. It reminds us that new Christians must be brought into the family of believers united under Jesus' lordship. They need to be included in our life together and upgraded from watchers to participants. The small groups we observed in our research often featured mutual accountability in the lives of their students. Jason, Thad, and Shea named their weekly small group Bible study with Nate as the most important ingredient in their Christian growth, largely because they were able to be honest with one another. They experienced a sense of gospel partnership through such a group. We think this makes sense. It's what friends do with friends: They exercise influence on one another. So instead of turning accountability into some kind of formal adult supervision, it needs to take on a natural—and more powerful—impact as adult mentors facilitate the process. People "like us" are less easily dismissed when they remind us of our obligations to Christ. The boys identified above practiced these kinds of relationships with one another because they were friends, and their adult leader, Nate, had given them a structure to express their faith in honest and personal ways.

"Teaching them to obey" is an agenda much too large to be carried solely by the few adult Bible experts hanging around young people. Most of us are imprecise combinations of teacher and learner.

Students are no different.

We teach while we learn. We teach unintentionally. And we're exposed to learning opportunities every day. We quickly learn that our obedience gets worked out in the middle of life's routines—at family dinner tables, recreational softball leagues, class breaks, and in endless other situations. The most effective teaching for that kind of obedience is life-on-life coaching. We end up *showing* each other how to live—even when we don't intend to. God expects us to teach each other in these natural venues "while going." The many *one anothers* of Scripture make this clear. Students simply have more opportunities than adults for this sort of influence. For example, a student who decides not to cheat when test answers get passed to him can encourage his friends to take similar stands of integrity without saying a word. These student examples don't have to be flashy, but their influence shouldn't be minimized. The power of naturally living in Jesus is what makes for a compelling translation of how we participate in God's Big Change process. When students catch this vision, they can make an impact adults aren't naturally positioned to make.

That's why the first role of adult mentors is to possess a clear picture of how a life is transformed by God. We need such a perspective if we want to understand how we will coach students into naturally fruitful friendships.

ADULTS SHOULD...Be clear-minded about how teens grow into courageous and contagious followers of Jesus Christ. When we focus on *natural principles* of transformation, God will work through us to launch students with integrity who can be influential leaders among their friends.

FLEX FOCUS 2:
SHOW ME THE WAY

Have you ever wondered how this personal commitment thing works with students? What forces are at work when someone decides to follow Christ-in-you? It's fascinating to see how Jesus inspired his dedicated following by first offering his life and example to the disciples. He pioneered a servant-leader selflessness that won the hearts of his team. He shared every part of his life with the Twelve, and by doing so imprinted an example of godliness in their lives.

Our research gave us the chance to listen to groups discussing their motivations to become student leaders. The teens in our study repeatedly identified the inspirational example of the youth worker leading the group. These adults were in front of the pack, showing their teens what was expected. Youth groups often seemed to take on the personality of their adult leaders. These adults were clear in their ministry philosophy, operated confidently with their leadership team, designed the programs for the group, and created the atmosphere for youth ministry gatherings. And they were deeply appreciated for their efforts.

Our surveys asked students to identify persons who were most helpful to their personal evangelism efforts. More than 22 percent identified youth pastors as most helpful. These students came from homes where evangelism was likely never observed. In fact, 80 percent of the students surveyed had either never or seldom seen a parent lead someone to Christ. Only 3.5 percent cited their parents as most influential in their efforts to lead others to Christ. This doesn't necessarily mean their parents didn't do evangelism. But it *does* mean students weren't seeing it. In effect, these student leaders were being asked to do something they never watched their parents practice, even though the majority of them had grown up in a Christian home.

There were a few students, however, who told us that their parents were the most helpful to their peer outreach efforts. They reported seeing their parents lead *their* friends to Christ almost monthly. For these students, those windows of observation played a huge role in helping them reach their friends for Christ.

The impact of modeling is reflected even more significantly in another one of our findings. When student leaders saw adults lead someone to Christ at least weekly, they reported leading more than eight friends to Christ themselves. If they observed adults evangelizing only monthly, student leaders were likely to lead fewer of their friends (four to eight) to Christ. Our research showed this to be a consistent trend. *The more often adults were observed leading others to Christ, the more often student leaders led their own friends to Christ.* When adults engaged in observable evangelistic practices less frequently, student leaders followed their pattern. The students who reported seeing adults only occasionally—if ever—evangelize were also likely to report not having led anyone to Christ.

There's one other significant nugget from our research regarding the impact of modeling on student-peer evangelism. Students who saw other students lead peers to Christ were dramatically more effective in their own evangelism efforts than those who didn't benefit from such examples. Of the students who had helped friends come to Christ, 85 percent said they had seen an adult lead someone to Christ, and 85 percent of *those* students had seen a teen lead a teen to Christ. *All of the students who were most effective in helping friends come to Christ had seen other teens lead a peer to faith.* Evangelistically fruitful student leaders certainly follow modeled behavior.

So which is it? Should adults model evangelism or should teens? *Yes.* Research makes the case for the power of modeling at all levels. Mentoring adults should model outreach because young people need to be shown how to do it and convinced that it's important. But they should always have an eye on which students could be developed into even more effective models. It is these students who will ultimately prove most influential on other Christian peers.

After such encouraging reports it might be surprising to learn that even the top student leaders in our research identified fear as the number one obstacle to their evangelistic efforts. Fear can undermine even the sharpest youth minister's planning and training—no less a student's.

We interviewed a student named James about what it would take to open the door to lead a peer to Christ. He was fearful because he didn't want to alienate the friend and be rejected. He went on to list all of the evangelism training in which he had participated with his youth group. "At every monthly meeting we go out to share in teams. Once you learn how to share, it's your own," he said. Later in the interview James described the role a mission trip had played in his life: "I learned how to serve. I love being behind the scenes." Even though this student was skilled and experienced in evangelism and had seen others lead friends to Christ, he'd never personally played what he considered a key role in helping a friend come to Christ. The main obstacle for him was his fear, and exposure to good training wasn't enough to help him overcome the barrier.

While it's important to teach students how to explain their faith, adults would be wise to devise methods to help student leaders move past their fears of sharing Christ. Simply challenging teens to become overcomers through inspirational talk is likely as short-lived as a coach's locker-room speech at halftime. Initial enthusiasm withers quickly in the face of hulking opponents who want to hurt you. Yet many adults who see themselves as directors of youth ministry take such a strategy.

Adult mentors should choose long-term strategies that help their student leaders both acknowledge and overcome their fears. Youth for Christ's 3Story approach encourages each of us to reduce one source of fear by working through natural, not contrived, conversations and relationships. Our own relationships with students can help them move through their witnessing fears when we model courage ourselves. Kent is one youth worker who is effective as an adult mentor and role model, due partially to the fact that he knows the fear of rejection but doesn't let it deter him from evangelizing. Bravery inspires bravery.

Have you ever wondered how the disciples overcame their fears? We know they had them, yet the contrast between their fearfulness in the gospels and their boldness in Acts is striking. How powerful it must have been to be eyewitnesses of the greatest act of sacrifice humanity has ever known! They understood the real fears of Jesus reflected in his prayer in Gethsemane the night he was arrested. The apostle John must have had the image-example of our Lord Jesus in mind when he wrote, "There is no fear in love. But perfect love drives out fear" (1 John 4:18a).

Adults who share both their lives and examples with their student leaders will find themselves inspiring commitments from those same teens. As this transformational life exchange takes place, it is perfectly natural for teens to look toward those significant adults when they need support in sharing their faith. That's one way Kent keeps busy sharing the gospel with teens.

His student leaders know they can trust him if they bring their friends to him to hear about Jesus. Thus, adults demonstrate their caring in yet another way: By making themselves available to explain Christ to teens' friends.

ADULTS SHOULD…Accept the responsibility of being a significant, and initial, model of evangelistic faithfulness to their students. By doing so, adults will mentor students by demonstrating how to overcome fear in presenting the gospel and inspire imitation. They'll also make themselves trustworthy and available resources to emerging student leaders who overcome their fears by asking their friends to talk to someone other than themselves about Jesus. Young people will be drawn to emulate the courageous and contagious faith they experience. Eventually, adults must demonstrate mentoring flexibility when they yield the primary modeling responsibility to students who, because of modeling dynamics, will be *exponentially* more effective than adults ever could be.

As we'll learn in Chapter 6, students in our study who seldom invited their friends to talk to adults about Jesus didn't reach any of their friends for Christ. When students more frequently invited non-Christian friends to talk to an adult, they were likely to see their friends come to Christ. These students see adults as partners in their evangelistic enterprise, a view no doubt inspired by the loving, sharing initiative visible in these mentors' lives.

There is an intersection of effectiveness that can be explored when our research results are considered in light of biblical truth. Modeling works because it reflects how we learn. It shouldn't surprise us to see Jesus employing this truth. He appointed the Twelve to "be with him" as they learned to preach the gospel (Mark 3:14). Disciples of Jesus are ultimately those persons who follow him—and other exemplary models—toward Christ-likeness. While it is clear that Paul wanted to help persons imitate Christ (Philippians 2:5), it is important to see that he offered himself as an accessible—though imperfect—pattern to help them on their way (1 Corinthians 11:1; Philippians 4:9). Paul even gushed about the domino effect of his modeling among the Thessalonians and beyond (1 Thessalonians 1:5-9). We adults can inspire such a following by ensuring that our love for students compels us to be available examples of courageous, contagious living. If, like Paul, we press on in our own faithfulness to Jesus, sharing our lives will help our students step up to new—and rewarding—levels of commitment.

FLEX FOCUS 3:
UP CLOSE AND PERSONAL

As we adult mentors come alongside students, we can get an up-close perspective of their spiritual needs and preparedness. Jesus gained such insight with his disciples because he lived with them. He knew, for example, that they weren't ready to deal with the forecast of his upcoming death until they understood better who he really was (Matthew 16:13-21). Peter's reaction demonstrated even then that the Lord still had his work cut out for him in preparing the disciples for what was to come (Matthew 16:22-23). Most of us won't have such extensive "life together" opportunities with our student leaders. What can we do to ensure that we're close enough to really know what's going on in their efforts to walk courageously with God and live faith contagiously with their friends?

Our study showed that regular accountability meetings with adult mentors not only help student leaders grow, but also lead to greater success for students trying to influence their friends for Christ. The majority of students who were evangelistically effective met regularly with adults; those who reported having no impact on their friends coming to Christ did not. During these meetings adults got to know students while offering general spiritual guidance. It was also likely that these mentoring adults used the time to probe specific areas of student leaders' lives and pray with them.

As an aside, we found that if students had these same types of meetings with their parents, the impact was not as significant. This may be because the nature of the meetings with parents focused on informal opportunities for nurture and care rather than those more intentional meetings organized to accomplish a youth ministry's focus of influence on others.

With the exception of those students who had helped more than eight friends become followers of Christ, youth pastors were rarely the adults identified as leading these one-on-one times. Youth pastors typically orchestrated an environment where mentoring adults could come alongside students. Regardless of the form that the mentoring meeting has, the influence adults have in the lives of the students by meeting with them helped them to grow in their relationship with Christ and lead their friends to Christian faith.

Note also that the role of these adult coaches in the lives of students is focused, not on evangelistic task performance, but on life growth and accountability. This doesn't mean evangelistic coaching is not part of this natural accountability structure. On the contrary students who were coached at least monthly on how to share their faith were dramatically more effective in reaching their peers for Christ than those who did not receive such coaching. However this evangelistic coaching was done in the context of a larger purpose to become faithful in all of life, not just skilled in a particular task.

Retreats and mission trips are practical ways to launch "in-your-life" coaching and life-assessment. Teens in our study consistently identified such time-intensive experiences with adults as milestones in their Christian life. This should come as no surprise. Wilderness camping or trips that are physically demanding and stressful are effective for ministry because they help strip away pretense and expose the true depth of one's character. An astute adult walking alongside a young man who has been sufficiently humbled by a mission trip's challenges is in the best position to see his needs for Christian growth and respond insightfully. Good coaches know their team well and craft their strategies accordingly.

As adult mentors draw near to student leaders, they will inevitably gain a position to influence how the young people use their time. Should students focus their limited energy on managing and planning youth ministry programs? Our findings suggest that this is a role best left to adults. We are committed to the idea that students ought to be ruthless in their focus, aiming to grow in their maturity and faithfulness to Jesus Christ. Feedback and planning in youth ministry are important aids to adult leaders, but they shouldn't be the focus of a formal student leader team. Most of the youth groups in our study centered their ministries on a philosophy similar to that of one ministry: "Love God. Love others. Love the lost." The research team heard different versions of that phrase at quite a few sites. Groups that were highly concerned with honoring God, loving each other, and witnessing to the lost were effective in reaching others for Christ. This evangelistic effectiveness dropped off among groups that asked their best teens to invest themselves in directing their youth ministry's programs.

There was virtually no relationship between a student's involvement in planning an event and any specific evangelistic behavior. Further, event planning didn't correlate with church involvement or other spiritual benefits in any significant way! If a student leader spends much time planning events, there is less likelihood that he will fall into the category of student leaders who reach more friends for Christ, pray more, or are more involved in their church.

So while we adults should look for ways to increase the confidence of student leaders through responsible delegation, it doesn't follow that program planning and management is a good time investment for our teens. We contribute to the trust that exists between ourselves and our student leaders when *we* provide programming that gives them confidence that the meetings will be socially safe and relevant to the world for the friends they invite.

Let's be clear: We're not advocating that student leaders stay away from programs. But we have to free them from unnecessary, energy-diffusing burdens. We want to help students concentrate their focus on the integrity that comes from courageous living and the influence that flows from a contagious faith. When we ask them to invest significantly in program leadership, we may do so at the expense of their ability to live large and impact their friends. A further discussion of how adults should respond to the program needs for student leadership will follow in Chapter 4.

How should student leaders learn what is expected of them? The youth ministers in our study took initiative to be clear in communicating those expectations. These adult mentors also used the Bible to teach students what God expects of them. This finding tips us off to yet another key role adults are to play in developing students who influence others.

Every group we visited reported that adult leaders supplied strong Bible teaching for their student leaders. Not only so, but student leadership was well organized and purposefully designed to accomplish all of the ends described here—including Bible study. The organizational efforts of these groups were striking. The stable, established structures provided a consistent environment where adult mentors and student leaders knew their roles and where effective, purposeful teaching took place on a regular basis.

Was there any pattern to the Bible content learned? We heard three predominant biblical themes that the students in our study reported learning from their adult leaders. The first theme was the challenge to demonstrate purity and integrity. They were taught that an obedient life needs to be demonstrated in their friendships, dating relationships, and decision-making. A second theme was to urge students to boldly share the good news of Christ. It reinforced the reason why these groups were successfully reaching other teens. They teach that evangelism is important in a myriad of ways. The third theme was that teens should allow God to work in their lives by practicing the kind of self-denial Jesus asked of his followers. Taken together, these themes are well described by the vision of students whose character is *courageous* and faith is *contagious*.

Some enterprising youth leaders are going to work on their PowerPoint presentations even now. That would be a mistaken application of this focus. Mentors are effective, not because their teaching is worthy of an iPod download, but because it is up close and personal. It is rooted in real-time relationships and informed by real-life issues. It is resistant to cultural shifts. Time after time we see Jesus' authority as a teacher catalyzed by his ability to paint on a life canvas shared by everyone. He referenced the tax-heavy occupation of the Roman army; the shallow, thorny, rocky, and good soils where farmers toiled; the corruption of religion in Jerusalem; and the fisherman's work on the Sea of Galilee. His were not classes you could skip, pick up the notes later, and not miss anything. We can only imagine how many times a bystander would have said, "You should have been there!" in reference to a dynamic learning experience with Jesus. Even more powerful would be the testimony of those who were the direct targets of his life coaching. They would line up to bear witness to the surprising life-change that came of their interaction with Jesus during the most common routines: Martha would never keep house the same way (Luke 10:38-41); Zacchaeus would never collect taxes the same way (Luke 19:1-10); a Samaritan woman with a trail of wrecked relationships would never draw water from the well in the same way (John 4).

ADULTS SHOULD…

Understand and expand the levels of trust students have for them through weekly coaching-accountability structures, consistent Christ-honoring programs, and confidence-building delegation. In addition, adults should take advantage of experientially powerful events, such as retreats and mission trips, to observe the learning levels of faith integration that have taken root in the lives of their young people. Finally, adult mentors must provide a regular diet of customized instruction from God's Word that will help students grow into leadership maturity, forming a courageous character and a contagious faith.

Adult mentors teach students from the Bible, determining what should be taught because they're up close and personal. By sharing life together we can naturally and knowingly inspect teens' gaps in maturity and faithfulness. Armed with these insights, it's pretty simple to teach toward students' most immediate learning needs.

FLEX FOCUS 4:
THE ART OF THE CHALLENGE

Teams can be a powerful, socializing force in helping students effectively reach their friends for Christ. Significant influence is possible when a group of students is dedicated to impacting their friends and schools for Jesus Christ. Adult leaders and mentors pay close attention to their most important values and then organize a structure that effectively holds the group accountable to those values. Obviously evangelistic faithfulness was one such common value among the groups we studied. Forming a core leadership group also seemed to be a crucial part of each group's Master Influence Plan.

We also noticed that the groups were well set up to receive and act upon challenges that would increase their faithfulness, especially with regard to reaching out to others. They seemed to support one another in risk-taking. Creativity was their standard as they brainstormed ways to meet new evangelistic opportunities. They rarely seemed to shrink from the next challenge. For these healthy student-leader teams, the question was seldom "Should we?" but more commonly "How should we?" One group verbalized the liberation of this type of thinking when it asked, "How should we spend a week together in the summer?" rather than assume that it would simply go to the camp it always attended. This openness led them to explore evangelistic possibilities. By the time their youth director suggested they should try to win a small town for Christ by taking their "camp" into the community for a week, the team was eager to respond to the challenge.

Didn't Jesus capture the imagination (and hearts!) of his followers by calling them to great acts of faith? "You give them something to eat," he told the disciples when they wondered if it wasn't time to send the large crowd away so they could grab some grub (Mark 6:37). He invited Peter to join him for a water-surface stroll when the big fisherman showed interest in taking the plunge (Matthew 14:29). Zacchaeus responded to Jesus' wild challenge to radically alter his lifestyle when he announced his new wealth distribution plan at dinner (Luke 19:8). Instance after instance in the gospels illustrates that Jesus continually stretched his followers, challenging them to become what they never dreamed possible.

The adults we saw in our study realized how creative challenges powerfully shaped the lives of these top students. As clear-minded mentors, they were well positioned by their caring, open lives. And knowing their student-leader team as only one who walks among them can, their challenges were wonderfully placed: Just far enough out of reach to stretch their teens' faith, but not so far as to discourage responsiveness.

Adult leaders in our study often chose evangelistic training methods that felt like a stretch to the students involved. Kids got bumped out of their comfort zones while learning how important outreach is. Those who seemed most effective selected training efforts that would help kids develop their skills as verbal witnesses. Teens who can articulate their faith well are clearly set apart from the crowd.[1] And there is evidence that verbal explanations of the gospel by friends are particularly significant for teens that come from irreligious backgrounds.[2] For most of us talking to lost friends about Jesus falls into the Challenge Zone. It's not surprising that our research showed that as students grew in their ability to explain to friends how to have a relationship with Jesus, they experienced success in seeing their friends become Christians. Evangelism Explosion, 3Story, and Dare 2 Share are three approaches frequently identified by ministries to train students in verbal witnessing skills. These training efforts—while offered regularly—usually took place at a time distinct from either the main youth group meetings or the student leader-team meetings. The success these students and ministries realized in seeing teens come to Christ was attributed in large part to this extra training. Calling students to step up to this new level of participation clearly was a challenge.

We shouldn't lose sight of the importance of challenging young people to do more when they aren't doing enough, or to do better when their efforts are poor. Mentors earn the right to issue such challenges. If we have a clear picture of what students can become in Christ, if they know we care about them and therefore trust us, and if we're close enough to understand what they need most in their next step of growth, it is wrong for us *not* to seek to influence them. This adult role is well done—almost naturally done—by mentors who come alongside students to coach them in courageous and contagious faith living.

Jesus was especially adept at delivering challenges to his disciples through appropriate delegation (he knew what they were ready for) and sensitive problem-posing (he stretched them to expand their understanding, not to embarrass them). We're smart if we ask the Lord to teach us more about his style as we seek to stretch students into leaders.

One of the strong and conclusive implications of this chapter is the likelihood that many of us will need to multiply the number of adult mentors involved in our youth ministries. For example, very few adults in our study met weekly with more than two student leaders. The real-life, real-time nature of mentoring—complete with its emphases on showing the way and being up close and personal—necessitates a tremen-

ADULTS SHOULD…
Stay alert to the transformational power of their student leaders' natural life agenda so they can challenge students to greater depth, provoke students to deeper reflection, and stimulate students to more thorough integration. It's abundantly clear this type of adult influence won't take place if there isn't a shared life context that encourages ongoing life accountability, a feature of mentoring.

dous investment of time. Nothing says "God loves you" quite as well as incarnating that truth. Given its clear derivation from the ministry of Jesus, there remains a pressing question for all of us who seek to raise students into leadership:

Why would we ever think we could bypass a mentoring approach and still help students acquire a courageous and contagious faith?

CHAPTER THREE
READY OR NOT

The count to 100 seemed quicker than it should have been, but the person who was "it" was counting by fives. All of the others were standing by, having hidden in their respective spots, as "Ready or not, here I come!" echoed in the dark backyard. The seemingly magical phrase sharpened attention and signaled a new reality—the hunt was on.

Anything could happen in this game of hide-and-seek.

There are moments in youth ministry that feel similar. We don't often get a beneficial "ready or not" as we work with adolescents who seem to change daily. Life doesn't pause to say, "Hey, this is a new reality" as we come alongside and listen to teens. We have to be able to spot those levels of readiness and the barriers that students confront along the way. And as the question echoes, we must look at those we're leading and respond appropriately based on their levels of readiness. Which of the following "ready or not" moments seem fresh and familiar to you?

- Those students who once were little children running around the church foyer suddenly appear on the doorstep of your ministry as middle schoolers.

- You challenge your middle school students to share their faith with their friends, but their eyes dilate and shift side to side to check out others' reactions.

- A family calls you at 1 a.m. Their son was just dropped off after his DUI arrest and accident, and they can't seem to restore peace in their home. They ask you to come help them.

- A large, enthusiastic group of freshmen enter your ministry, ready to do whatever is necessary to follow the Lord faithfully, but they seem unable to follow through for a variety of reasons, most time-related.

- An outreach event you've planned sees a dramatic swell of students, particularly a handful that you've been hoping would attend. And you're speaking.

Those are more obvious, but what about other ways that being ready intersects with youth ministry? Read the following and think through how readiness might be part of the problem:

- Nick seems distracted during the middle school group meetings, talking and restless. His mood swings can be pronounced, yet he shows up each week and can recite back to you almost every lesson you've taught!

- Daryl, an eighth-grader, says he doesn't enjoy worship music and just stands there with his buddies, who also aren't singing.

- As a freshman student leader, Lydia says she wants to reach her friends, but after a few months she stops showing up for the monthly training meetings.

- A.C. suddenly seemed to blossom spiritually during his junior year and became a strong leader within your group. He once barely seemed interested in leading, but now he seems wired for it!

Ask any veteran youth worker who has attempted to lead his or her students toward evangelistic purposes, and they will tell you that not all students are capable of responding the same. We may, with good intentions, try to give all students an equal chance to assume leadership roles. We want students to step up, to take the initiative and act on their own. Some clearly cannot. The issue is that they just aren't ready. Yet.

Is this okay? Or do we push the process? The latter question may seem to have an obvious answer to most readers, but those quick and confident answers may differ from the others. We're about to mix the evangelism research with some developmental realities; the results will cause us all to reconsider how development intersects with our leadership initiatives. One of the great hopes we have for ongoing research is that youth ministry will collectively continue to take a giant step forward in both faithfulness and effectiveness.

LETTING LEADERSHIP MATURE

Among the practical questions veterans of student leadership have learned to consider is whether age restrictions should be placed on those who will assume roles of leadership among their peers.

We would suggest there's a natural growth curve to leadership that cannot be rushed. If students aren't able to lead, the reason isn't always a matter of their desire, purity, or integrity—it could simply be due to developmental issues and a lack of clear vision for what we expect of them. This potential misdiagnosis is one of the reasons that we've identified courageous hearts and contagious faith as the target we'd wish for *all* young people who follow Christ. Leaders emerge from a pool of empowered students as God gifts them and as they are ready.

André is an example of the type of student leader who can confound us in this area. As a high school freshman he was enthusiastic, intent to learn, and energetic in his passion. He had a contagious personality that dripped with natural charisma. Because he laughed often at himself without a hint of cockiness, students who were older than André not only enjoyed him—they seemed to be carried along by the genuineness of his Christian life.

Would you include him or exclude him from your student leadership team? Some are puzzled that there is any debate at all in this decision. "What's to exclude?" you may be asking. And, in this true anecdote, the only caution we offer is to wonder whether some adolescents are developmentally ready for the responsibilities of peer leadership.

André hit a wall, and it rocked him so much that he never regained the confident influential stride of his youth. It's tough to isolate the causes of his fall from leadership ranks. He endured a lot of cruelty from classmates, something he tried to overcome by pushing himself toward success. Certainly being turned down by girls as he made his first attempts into the world of teenage dating didn't help. His heroes fell, a close friend died, and his first significant romantic relationship, which included sexual exploration, ended in disappointment and pain.

Some may protest that André's experience can't be described as normal for everyone. We agree. There are teens who have it much tougher and others who practically dance through their adolescent days. To be sure, many of our difficulties come from our own choices. But many do not, and the reality that life can be unpredictably difficult is so central to our human journey that we must do everything we can to equip young people with the hope and faith in Jesus Christ they need. How will they learn this great lesson about life's difficulties? Only experience can be counted on to deliver this message, and she is such a dispassionate tutor that we'd better strategically position ourselves to support our youth as they plunge into their course of study.

That's why some may hesitate to include freshmen (or younger) on their student leadership teams. There's no real substitute for testing someone's faith through the fire of tough experiences before they land on a pedestal of leadership expectations. *Don't underestimate the significant role learning through experience plays in the life of a student leader.*

Let's think of the leadership development process in an organic way, say in comparison to an apple tree. The tree may have a bunch of apples in the summer, each growing well and in full view, revealing the reality that there will be some good eating later in the year. Each fruit is clearly an apple, with all of the characteristics apples possess, but their green color and small size show that they haven't matured yet—they aren't ripe. They have the same substance, but the quality is different. In a similar way, you may see the makings of a future leader in your younger students. They may have the characteristics leaders need, and you can see their potential for significant future influence among their peers. However, as you move close enough to inspect, you can begin to see that the quality, consistency, and maturity have yet to develop—and development often happens only through experience.[3]

UNDERSTANDING LEADERSHIP

There's another issue here—our clear vision for what we mean by leadership. A considerable amount of research has shown us that despite the myriad of books, seminars, and conferences on the topic, there are inconsistent definitions of leadership. One of the tripping points for youth workers is to confuse temperament and personal characteristics as leadership qualities. Leadership is more than just being outspoken or having a father or mother on the church board. It is intertwined with other developmental factors. As the leaders of 4-H found: "Leadership development is a multi-faceted, complex process which involves growth and attainment in leadership knowledge, attitudes, skills, and aspirations. In order to actually develop leadership in beyond-the-family settings such as school or 4-H, youth must be ready physically, emotionally, cognitively, and socially."[4]

Leadership requires knowledge, competency, and character.[5] Even if a student is coached by a caring, effective adult youth worker, he or she will need to reflect on past actions, communicate clearly, act with consistency, and make choices relatively free from peer influence.[6] It shouldn't confound us, then, that middle schoolers have difficulty consistently stepping out from their friends to take leadership roles or even to demonstrate their faith in Christ. These aren't college students who have endured trials such as learning to drive, navigating dating conversations, enduring a few failures, showing up for a regular job, or reflecting on and adjusting to post-high school career or college directions.

One way youth workers have attempted to work around younger students' inexperience and immaturity and still use a leadership-as-influence approach is to look for "gatekeeper" students, popular students who are leaders because other students already follow them.[7] That was part of the selection process with André. However, he clearly was not yet a leader with influence—he was a popular kid with a dynamic personality who was early in the ripening process.

There are three questions to kick around as you think about the readiness of particular students to assume leadership roles:

1. Are they ready to respond?

2. Can they effectively navigate the sociocultural influences of an often cynical social world at school, work, and with friends?

3. What prominent developmental aspects are in process in their lives?

A RESPONSIVE HEART

In the first chapter we discussed how our hearts shape us, that this is where the action is. As my (Terry) daughter was learning to play volleyball, a college coach took her aside and reminded her that while coaches could teach her all of the skills necessary to play, coaches "can't teach heart." The coach knew there are limits to each player's natural ability, moments when they will feel like giving up, and situations when players must dig down and find determined commitment to getting better. Similarly, despite the best plans, warm relational styles, and veteran expertise of youth leaders, students have to be responsive to be ready.

Different from the performance nature of sports (and life), having a contagious faith is primarily connected to being someone different, a process that God does in our lives. As we'll see later, when students and adults live out that life in Christ in front of others, opportunities will arise to share the hope that they have (1 Peter 3:15). If we invert the process and push ripening students before they're ready to respond well…it's like pushing a volleyball player to play before she develops the muscles to hit and play well. After repeated failure at hitting or serving, the net will seem large and quitting an attractive solution.

Another facet of responsiveness is that adult leaders often confuse temperament with leadership ability. We like the upfront students who can captivate students with humor and the captains of sports teams whose commanding ways can marshal others into action. Responsiveness is about desire, something coaches can't instill but that they can model.

Laura and Christie were sisters whose commitment to quality and steady helpfulness made them valuable members of a dynamic evangelistic leadership team. They didn't exhibit the upfront skills others possessed, and they sleepily endured Sunday afternoon student leader meetings. But if you listened closely to their hearts, you knew they were responsive to what God was doing and where he was leading them. Their consistent participation on the student leadership team showed their responsiveness to adult modeling and coaching. As they matured, their organizational skills, inviting natures, and consistent examples to make a difference naturally emerged, and they began to play key roles in others coming to Christ.

It was no surprise then that as they went off to college and further matured, they joined an evangelistic ministry, grew into leadership roles, and committed their post-college vocational lives to the purposes of reaching others with the gospel.

The local youth ministry of (the imaginary) Northern Community Church (NCC) has a group of eighth-grade students whom most youth workers would envy—numerous young teens with natural leadership skills oozing within their collective energy. This is one of those rare classes: A large group of students with off-the-chart potential, the kind of potential that has the attention of the community.

The temptation for NCC's youth pastor would be to begin immediately developing leadership training for preparing each student to lead when he or she enters the group as freshmen. However, if we could move in closer and listen to the students (and their parents), we would find that, despite the flashy potential (and we agree this is a rare and impressive group), each struggles intensely just to make it through each day. The students would tell you of struggles with friends, uncertainty if their faith is even real, deep unsettledness about who they are, and a fear of saying or doing anything out of line with what others are doing. Their basic responsiveness to God is in question as they try to understand the implications of this faith they're developing.

Yet they come to every youth ministry event. And give no hint that they're on such unsure footing.

While we youth workers are tempted to think program-matically when we view student groups like the one at NCC, as we inspect the lives of adolescents more closely, we quickly observe the developmental issues at play. And they often take priority whether we want them to or not. Consequently, once a student desires to be responsive to God, he or she still has to develop the ability to lead in a pressure-packed social environment.

NAVIGATING THE SOCIOCULTURAL WORLD

Despite our symbiotic relationship with technology, there are significant differences between humans and machines. We are born into a world of people, and that social environment is more powerful than we imagine. There is debate regarding the extent to which socialization influences our actions and behaviors. Some would say it's significant (how else can you explain why so many of us male youth workers have goa-tees?) while others would point to developmental research that says we can navigate peer influences with ease.

If you watched the eighth-grade group from NCC from a distance, you'd observe students who participate in almost every extracurricular group at school. Most are at the top of their class, and they collectively exhibit a dynamic presence during worship times at Wednesday-night services. Yet as you listen to them individually, you'd hear social panic: Fear that they are out of step with others, that close friendships seem suddenly in peril, and that they just can't find their way. They're going through each day outwardly humming with col-lective positivity, but unable to step out on their own due to a high level of uncertainty of how to do that in a social world.

Social scientist David Elkind's concept of the "imaginary audience" is a powerful way to describe how teens' devel-opment may affect their relationships.[8] Young people move through their day convinced that their peers are always watching—no, *scrutinizing*—them. This adolescent egocentrism has a natural consequence on their relationships. How could a perspective that essentially reorders the world so that everything revolves around a person *not* have a considerable impact? More specifically, great numbers of teens live daily with a kind of terror that their watching peers will discover flaws that will possibly make them social lepers.

Some have observed that the older teens are, the less important it is to know that "everyone is watching."[9] Worrying less about what others may see in them means adolescents' susceptibility to peer influence drops (even though peer pressure rises) as they grow older.[10] So asking young teenagers, in a sea of peer influence with their own self-consciousness at its highest level, to lead can sometimes place them at risk socially—particularly if there is an internal and unseen struggle raging. You can begin to see why expecting younger adolescents to grasp dynamic leadership might be unrealistic.

Research affirms some cautions we need to think about with regard to younger teens. Some may simply care too much about what their friends think, making them more likely to try to please peers as they consider important choices affecting their Christian standards. We should be cautious when we decide which young teens are ready for student leadership responsibility. But we can also be confident that the influence of solid, older Christian teens can be profoundly effective on their younger friends.

LEADERS IN DEVELOPMENT

As students are tossed about in the social world around them, where are the places that might produce cracks in faith's foundation when life's inevitable storms come? We can think of at least three significant areas worth keeping an eye on as our young people lean into life: How students discover and construct their identity, how they choose to act, and how they learn. Though youth workers often see identity issues as the most significant for young people, each area has notable implications for how effective student leaders can be as they seek to influence their friends for Jesus Christ.

DEVELOPING AN IDENTITY

One of the great tasks we all negotiate as we grow up is discovering our self-identity. Though personality and temperaments are in place from their early years, teens need to learn who they are in relation to their friends and family. What value and conviction base will they develop from which their life's decisions will flow? What activities will aid or hinder this public identity pursuit? With what groups will they affiliate? Further, which ones would they say best represent them?

It's as if each of us sometime during our development is handed a blank canvas on which we are to paint the self-portrait we'll have to live with. There are some limitations in the drawing instruments available for our use, just as we can't make every choice related to our own identity formation. For example, we can't choose our biological families or the genetic code that has endowed us with a particular body, intelligence capability, or personality range. So, given these tools, what will teens create? Who will they become? What palette will they choose to paint from?

This painting of identity is just begun in the teenage years, and the final portrait is not well formed until the mid-20s. Even our upperclassmen are just beginning the brush strokes of identity construction. In recent years developmental science has pointed to the reality of "emerging adulthood" as an important stage in our life development.[11]

Researcher James Marcia expanded upon the pioneering psychosocial work of Erik Erikson to help us understand something of the process of identity formation. His research led him to conclude that adolescents must experience a sense of crisis before they make the commitment necessary for identity achievement. The nature of this crisis period varies considerably between individuals. Some teens may spend years in this state of bewilderment, suspending their identity commitment until they have settled key questions. Others move through some periods of questioning without slowing down much at all. Marcia suggests that anyone who wants to be successful in negotiating the key issues of their sense of identity must go through this moratorium. It takes a while for some while others move through this period quickly. It's as if we're in an identity holding pattern before we can land our self-plane safely.[12]

But Marcia's contributions also describe those who hit an important snag in their identity development. He uses the term "foreclosure" to identify young persons who make their identity commitment before experiencing the crisis that brings true ownership. This comes from truly wrestling with questions and issues so that choices genuinely become their own. Sometimes they simply want to please their family members or church, so their self-defining choices are, in a sense, corrupted. But these decisions aren't truly owned as their identity because they closed the deal prematurely. Most of our students leave their high school days with foreclosed identities.

These students are like the explorers who first mapped out climbing routes in the Grand Tetons. When starting their ascent toward the highest mountain in the range—following what looked like the most natural course—they climbed a few thousand feet before reaching a smaller summit that proved to be a dead end. There was no way to continue from this peak, so the mountaineers were forced to descend to the valley to figure out another way to climb to the top of the Grand. Fittingly, they named this smaller summit Disappointment Peak.

If experience-based exploration and crises are important to the task of identity formation, how should we understand younger adolescents who signal that they're ready to become student leaders? There's a chance they may be standing on identity's version of Disappointment Peak, confident they've arrived, yet unaware that they have a lot of climbing ahead of them. If we suspect this is the case, we're smart if we create some sort of leadership farm system, a place where teens can try on the commitments to student leadership that will help them in their necessary exploration.

We also don't want to rule out the possibility that some students really have been attentive to the identity options around them, truly have wrestled with soul-searching questions, and are genuinely ready to commit to following Jesus closely and influencing friends deeply. When we're satisfied that a young person fits this profile, it's time to rejoice. We've found a new ministry partner!

A page out of Jesus' coaching notes could really help us. He often invited casual followers to take a closer look. His parables rewarded those who were honestly hungry to apply his truth, separating them from the passive crowd of note-takers. When he chose the Twelve, he knew they'd had enough experience with him to make an informed choice to follow him in faith.[13] Their period of investigation (crisis?) had helped them to know that they were ready to make the commitment (identity achievement?) of becoming his disciples. And Jesus respected the importance of this developmental need enough that he constantly cautioned crowds against making popular, but premature, decisions to follow him. We shouldn't be surprised that Jesus was so developmentally savvy. He was, after all, a participating partner in designing our processes of identity formation.

LEARNING TO CHOOSE WISELY

There are at least two aspects to growth in the moral domain of life. The first has to do with principled decision making, and the second with acting on those convictions with right behavior. Just because a young person (or youth worker) has the right convictions doesn't mean that she or he will morally act on them. Of all the research on moral development, we'd like to focus on what may help us in our student leadership strategies.

The research in moral decision making has been dominated by the work of Harvard psychologist Lawrence Kohlberg.

He has attempted to evaluate decisions without making judgments about whether a choice is right or wrong. Instead, he assesses the quality of the thinking that goes into a decision. For that reason, Kohlberg would say that the best moral decisions aren't possible unless we are capable of the most thorough kind of analysis. Good thinking is necessary before we can make good decisions, moral or otherwise.[14]

Guess what? Young adolescents are just getting acquainted with their new brain package. Their capacity to think about hypothetical situations and possibilities is a relatively new development for them. That means, according to Kohlberg, they're limited in their moral decision-making processes because they're limited in their thinking. More specifically, they will typically decide that something is right or wrong on the basis of consequences ("It's only wrong if I get caught") or rules ("It's wrong if everybody says it's wrong") rather than principles ("It's wrong because it violates true ethical standards").

Maybe this limitation on the way kids make moral judgments should be important in choosing student leaders. If so, it should lead us to be doubly cautious when considering our youngest teens. But these issues don't have to matter the most to Christians when they consider moral growth. Kohlberg's work deals exclusively with *how* persons think about matters of right and wrong; we're at least as concerned with *what* they think.[15] We want kids to make the right moral choices and point to the Bible as the standard to guide us. In fact, there is evidence to suggest that post-adolescent Christians make moral decisions after filtering them through their most important commitment—their faith in Jesus Christ.[16]

If kids make the right choices because they are Christians, they may be in a good position to influence their friends for the Lord. That assumes, of course, that they actually live by their decisions. Actions speak louder than words. It's a disturbing reality that too often moral thinking does not necessarily lead to moral behavior.

The Link Institute of Huntington University initiated a series of research projects in an effort to peek into the moral choices of students in youth ministry groups. Their findings, and those of other research, offer a mixed review:

- About 64 percent of a sample of Midwestern students who made public commitments to sexual abstinence reported they were still living by that commitment at the end of a four-year period. In 2007 the national Youth Risk Behavior Survey noted that only 52 percent of American high school students are still virgins.[17] Is the difference worth celebrating?

- We identified 84 percent of those who made such a pledge and could still say they had not yet had sex in 1999.

- In the United Kingdom, 26 percent of teenagers reported having sexual intercourse before age 16.[18] In Canada slightly fewer than 25 percent reported having intercourse during their middle school days.[19] In the United States the percentage has been in decline, but the median age for first sexual intercourse is 16.9 years for girls and 17.4 years for boys. Half of American youth are sexually active in early adolescence.[20]

- An estimated half of men and women will have a sexually transmitted disease by the time they're 25 years of age.[21]

Such statistics practically beg us to help teens make important moral decisions as early as we can. But the reality is that there will be some slippage in their commitments due in part to warp speed developmental changes in young adolescents.

HELPING STUDENTS LEARN WELL

We started this chapter with some "ready or not" moments youth workers face. These scenarios offer just a few glimpses into youth ministry that make it one of our greatest ministry-leadership adventures. We've devoted our lives to it! Coming alongside young people in rapid growth presents some of the greatest joys and challenges, particularly as we factor in our responsibility to teach students along the way.

Seeing a student encounter the good news of Jesus Christ and choose to follow him is one of those moments when you see God's life-giving story at play in the world. Watching students grow into leadership roles with a contagious faith that impacts others' lives is one of the chief goals of ministry. That growth process requires a level of learning that is often missing in youth ministry. That's why some set up leadership teams: To help create an incubation process that provides a warm environment for growth to take place, a place where students can learn about leadership and taking responsibility for others. If we want students to assume responsibility for seeing friends come to Christ, we need to help them develop the capability and experience to make decisions that result in effective action. That requires a lot of knowledge!

This instructive challenge presents a repeated frustration, however, as we help adolescents take the first steps in spiritual leadership. We can teach, lead, coordinate, give them our best counseling moments, and still wonder whether they'll really ever get it. When students hesitate or seem unable, you may be tempted to chalk it up to their lack of responsiveness—or even laziness. We want to suggest that it may be a learning development issue—and we may need to adjust our teaching so that they can understand.[22]

One of the hottest subjects in current literature and media is adolescent learning. The field of social science pours out research each year, focused on how teens learn, how best to teach, and the psychology of the learning process. Maybe it's a response to the perceived rebellion and disinterest of students in school; maybe it's not. But scholars have spent considerable time examining effective learning practices for teachers to employ. Their work can benefit those of us in the youth ministry field as we try to help students learn and grow.[23]

The field of natural science has contributed to our understanding through research focused on the physical nature of the brain as it develops, as well as how its development intersects with and affects learning.[24] Popular art, through books and movies, has featured stories of master educators who take seemingly disinterested students and make learning come alive for them, producing impressive results. The implications from these three fields' work are that it *is* possible to educate students *if* we're willing to put the effort into learning how teens think and how their thinking matures, and respond through effective methods of teaching.

Students learn through a variety of avenues. They can learn through formal settings, including church, school, and sports practices. And they can learn through informal settings as they simply live, observing others and imitating them. In fact, they probably primarily learn through informal means— even about traditional school subjects.

As young people develop the capacity to act independently from others within their social setting (this is a lifelong pursuit), they obtain the ability to make reasoned decisions based on experience, reflection, and prediction. If a young teen's brain is still struggling to pay attention, hasn't developed a capacity for memory, and struggles to quickly organize information, it will be difficult for him or her to act consistently in a leadership role. You can see where the development of thinking intersects with a person's confidence and ability to share his faith.

Yet there is promise and hope. When responsible adult leaders enter into the lives of students, they can help students take initial steps toward new levels of responsibility and self-reliance. Because the chief way students learn is through modeling others (usually Christian adults), it's important that adults are caring enough to inspire and show the way for students. These models of contagious faith are the most powerful vehicles to fuel your leadership-development agenda. It follows that having immature adults who demonstrate less will impede your ability to develop leaders.

At the beginning of the chapter we told you about A.C., a kid with seemingly unlimited potential who struggled with leadership until he turned 16. Even though he had a 4.0 GPA and starred at three varsity sports, he wasn't able to put it all together until his junior year. Then he soared! How did he know what to do when the time came? He had watched the upperclassmen during his first two years in the youth ministry. He looked to his small group leader of the last two years. And he regularly met with his youth pastor, who had been waiting for the leadership potential pop. The youth pastor had been laying the healthy foundations necessary for A.C. to faithfully exercise all of his gifts. When everything clicked A.C. knew what leadership looked like because he'd been watching it in action for two years.[25]

What subjects are the lives of your adult leaders teaching? What are your students learning from your life? Are you all available for your students to get close to, to learn what difference Christ is making in your lives? Are you laying healthy foundations in their lives? If you and your volunteers are playing key roles in leading others to Christ, your students will follow your example. As we'll show you later, evangelistic modeling is a key part of ministries in which teens regularly reach other teens for Christ.

Given some of the social-science insights presented in this chapter, how will you vote on the issue of putting young teens to work as student leaders? Our suggestion is make sure the investment you make in these willing but youthful students is solid and thoughtful, but wait awhile before heavily depending on them. Don't be in a hurry to form courageous hearts or to coach contagious faith—focus on doing so well. By the time younger students reach their junior year, they—and you—will have a much more stable picture of the kind of person they really want to become and the kind of student leaders they were created to be.

CHAPTER FOUR
ADULTS AS PROGRAM PROVIDERS

We have primarily directed this book at Christian adults who want to invest in teens, hoping to maximize their development as followers of Christ who become contributors to God's mission and, ultimately, influential friends among their peers.

Yet some youth leaders who would agree with that end goal disagree on the methods to best achieve it. There are those who advocate strong student-led ministry strategies and suggest that adults need to retreat from the action so far that they are nearly invisible. With assumptions eerily similar to Rousseau's educational philosophy, they infer that the more successful we are at extracting adults from any involvement with teens, the more likely it is that teens will naturally grow like mountain wildflowers into their fullest potential.

At the other end of the spectrum is a vision of student ministry rooted in the adult-centered, modern approaches that spread aggressively in the 1960s and '70s. Adults with special training connect with adolescents through programs and relationships, interpreting the expectations of a faith journey for them and coaching them toward following Christ according to their particular faith tradition. It's our observation that this youth ministry model is still the dominant professional template driving most church hiring practices to this day.

We think there's a desirable middle road for adults, one that is more true to biblical ministry patterns and better fits the research observations we've made. First, we believe it only makes sense that adults in ministry with teens should leverage their gifts and wisdom in a way that is consistent with teachings about how the body of Christ builds itself up "as each part does its work" (Ephesians 4:16). Next, we'd like to urge adults to operate with the kind of deliberate, visionary restraint that actually empowers young people to step into greater responsibility for how their faith impacts their world.

A case has already been made for the most significant role of adults in this student leadership growth agenda. Adults must be relational mentors above all else, paying attention to the formation of students' hearts for Jesus while teaching their teens to do the same. As we observed in the last chapter, adults taking this lifeguard perch should be well informed of natural adolescent development and how it contributes to each teen's readiness to lead. Such judgments can be guided by general guidelines, but ought to be made on a case-by-case basis by adults who are up close and personal with their students.

The question of this chapter is: What range of strategies is available to adults who seek to empower students for courageous and contagious faith?

To begin the discussion we'd like to summarize a few convictions we bring to this particular question:

- All ministries should be person-centered, requiring a relational posture and heart-shaping expertise.

- *Formative experiences* include the sum total of everything—hidden, accidental, and deliberately orchestrated—that contributes to the transformation and/or malformation of people.

- *Socialization* explains the values-forming process at work when we naturally interact with our culture, the immediate environment, and people in general, especially those closest to us. It includes modeling dynamics and the intentional shaping of how learning is delivered.

- *Curricular plans* involve explicit designs of ordered learning experiences that include programs and informal, intentional activities with a beginning and end, defining the course to be run by students.

- *Programs* are formally scheduled gatherings of purpose, including regular routines and special events. They can—and ought to—be regularly reviewed, assessed, revised, and even dismissed as they are judged for their effectiveness at delivering their intended purposes and serving fundamental relational and transformational ministry goals.

- According to our research, asking students to invest time and energy in program design and implementation is counterproductive to the goal of positioning them for Christ-centered influence with their friends.

- A specific student-leader team strategy seems to be an effective way to raise up young people whose faith is courageous and contagious.

- Adult leaders are in the best position to structure relationships of accountability between students and other adults, cast vision through biblical teaching, and orchestrate meetings/activities (including retreats and other special events) to which young people can confidently invite their non-Christian friends.

Figure 1 illustrates the relationships between particular program strategies and general curricula, socialization, and experience. Each of these elements contributes to the range of strategic considerations available to adults who want to empower their students.

FIGURE 1

The desired relationship between program, curriculum, socialization, and formative experiences is that each is aligned to the same central purpose. We suggest that empowering students for courageous and contagious faith can serve to focus programs properly. When each element is aligned to the center, they reinforce one another, effectively concentrating the impact of all formation experiences like a laser locked on its target.

It is, of course, possible for programs to stand unaligned with their central purposes, curricular plans, or socialized values. When this happens, the processes of formation work against one another, reducing the likelihood that the desired transformation will take place. Figure 2 illustrates this un-aligned relationship between programs, curricula, socialization, and all other formative experiences. Notice that, while there is some intersection between all of the elements, it's possible to locate program strategies that aren't part of either the curricular plans or reinforced by the values to which students need to be socialized.

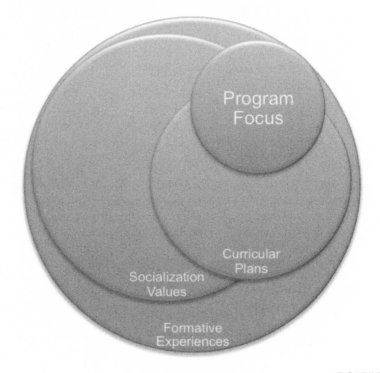

FIGURE 2

These sorts of program efforts can be malformational rather than transformational. For instance, when young people attend the annual four-day music festival for no other reason than because it's always been a part of the summer schedule, there's no guarantee that it will a) be an empowering experience,

b) fortify their hearts for a courageous faith, or c) contribute to their lifestyles as contagious and winsome followers of Jesus. Such outcomes may be possible, but their likelihood shouldn't be left to chance or the unrelated planning of festival promoters. What's required throughout the program, curricula, and socialization process is intentionality and vigilance on the part of the adult leaders, who have the up close and personal advantage of being relational mentors.

INTENTIONALITY

Here's why *intentionality* is one of our favorite words. It properly places the emphasis of our leadership behaviors where it ought to be: On our own deliberate faithfulness as stewards of the lives and ministries with which we've been entrusted. There is no guarantee that the outcomes we seek can be attained through our efforts. We simply do not get to control others' responses to our ministry initiatives. This is a humbling reality that ought to be learned sooner rather than later in one's ministry career, one that has been forcefully driven home every time we've given students exams over material that we were sure we taught well. But it's important to understand that just because we don't control the outcomes we seek in our students doesn't mean we shouldn't align and focus our efforts to maximize the likelihood of the results we hope for. As often as we make such adjustments, we are being intentional.

And to the degree that we understand and cooperate with God's design for bringing about transformation, we will offer more than our best intentions or motives. The expectations of our own faithfulness are informed by the degree of our own spiritual maturity. If we hope to lead our students well, we must take the journey ourselves with integrity.

If we want students' hearts to be courageous for the Lord Jesus, we need to be willing to break with many popular ministry practices and participate in the mission of God as Jesus taught.

If we want student's lives to carry a contagious faith, influencing their friends and families for the Lord Jesus, we need to focus ourselves on the leadership task of equipping others to live in the way of Jesus.

Intentionality is a value before it's a skill. It's a mindset of preparedness and a commitment to proactive action. Alert to opportunities and vigilant in safeguarding against threats, intentional adult leaders are in the best position to align the full range of formative experiences available to empower students for a courageous and contagious faith.

Given the premise of this book, let's assume that our main pursuit is passing the baton and multiplying the number of young leaders willing to join in the mission of God. Further, let's agree that such an outcome—if beyond our control—is within our reach as intentional adults faithful to the task God has given us. In order to align our support with such a goal, our first commitment must be to shape the socializing values that our young people experience. We want to bend our practices to cooperate with the transforming power of the Holy Spirit rather than ask God to bless our mess. Four biblical values are essential to the process that empowers students for courageous and contagious faith living. Ensuring that these values are thoroughly experienced in our shared life is a key role for adults, and a priority that precedes curricular planning or program selection.

SOCIALIZATION VALUES

PRAYER

Our prayer patterns[26] as adult leaders testify to how deeply we believe in its absolute necessity to accomplish the work to which we've been called. If the challenges of empowering students could be overcome by improved managerial skills or programmatic excellence, then prayer would be a perfunctory exercise of religious obligation. Jesus' own words are a reminder that the need for co-workers—the kind of teen allies we hope to cultivate—are met as we pray to the Lord of the harvest (Luke 10:2). Before he chose his own 12 "student leaders," he bathed his decision in prayer (Luke 6:12-19).

Can students' hearts become courageous or their faith contagious without the active work of the Holy Spirit? When we pray we solicit God's intervention and put ourselves in position to understand what he's up to in the lives of our teens.

We're in good company when we devote ourselves to prayer as a means to accomplish the transformation of young people into influential leaders. Paul labored to cultivate followers who were imitators of Jesus, and a significant part of his work toward that end was prayer (Galatians 4:19; Colossians 1:24-2:8). He prayed that God would give the Ephesians understanding of important mysteries critical to their faith (Ephesians 1:17-19; 3:14-19). And Jesus made it clear that the disciples couldn't minister effectively without prayer (Mark 9:28-29).

One additional indicator of this value is the frequency and detail with which we ask others to pray. By soliciting specific prayers, often from teams of people, we acknowledge our dependence on God to accomplish what we can't do on our own. This humility needs to be an observable pattern, a way of life modeled for our students. If the apostles needed wisdom and grace enough to covet the prayers of others, so should we. (See Acts 8:26-40; 10; 12:5-12; Romans 15:30; 2 Corinthians 1:8-11; Ephesians 6:18-20; Colossians 4:2-4; 1 Timothy 2:1; James 1:5-6.)

LOVE

The love of God is an amazing, incomprehensible foundation of our faith. It is undeserved, inescapable, and transformational (John 3:16; Romans 5:8; 8:31-39). All who come into contact with it—especially those, like teens, who hunger for meaningful relationships—can expect to be changed.

Some of the student ministries in our research project described themselves by attractive, but tame social goals such as "friendly" or "warm." We ought not to settle—and dare not domesticate—the experiences visiting teens have with their Christian friends. God's love is a force to be reckoned with; the most creative of programs can't begin to match its impact in the life of a young person. This is one of the key roles of adults: To ensure that divine love is unleashed throughout their ministries. All other strategies must be ordered to deliver—rather than dilute—this penetrating and life-altering love.

Those of us who are identified as his children are to be emissaries of this love. It is to be evident in our lives as we engage one another and the world (Romans 13:8; James 2:5-10; 1 John 3:11-18). It's how, as Jesus said, a watching world will know we are Christians (John 13:34-35).

One implication of God's love is that we are to build a nurturing community where an empowering foundation is given to young people (Ephesians 3:16-19; Philippians 1:9-11). The more diverse these environments, the more dramatic the testimony of how divine love smashes social barriers and infuses inexplicable hope into our life together (Acts 2:42-47; Galatians 5:2-15; 1 Thessalonians 4:9-12). No wonder the Great Commandment is an acknowledged priority for Christians. When people who are contagious with the love of Jesus surround a teen, extraordinary change can be expected (Mark 12:28-34). Love fills the once feeble hearts of otherwise normal students with courage, fortifying their resolve to take any and every risk necessary to follow the Lord Jesus Christ.

And this love—if it is truly derived from God—must not be housed under the lock and key of our student ministry home locales. The love of God can't be sequestered, but must be released to change families, neighborhoods, schools, and the entire world. Jesus reminded those who questioned his actions with Zacchaeus that he came to "seek and save" the lost (Luke 19:1-9). Young people can't catch the vision of faith-contagious living without recognizing that, by taking initiatives with their friends and actually pursuing them in love, they follow the pattern of Jesus and represent him well (John 20:21; 2 Corinthians 5:14).

GOD'S WORD

Against a postmodern youth landscape characterized by relativism, experientialism, and distrust of authority outside of self, we want to take a stance and align with another transcendent value. The Scriptures have been provided so that we might live enlightened by their truth. In fact, without access to the revelation of God's Word, we're impoverished as we seek to conform our own lives and direct our students in the way of Jesus.

Our Lord himself indicates that the way of life he is describing is not easily attainable, in part because there are false teachers who distract us from seeking the will of God. But Jesus punches up the Sermon on the Mount with a killer finish, offering a parable asserting that persons who build their lives around hearing and practicing his words will be able to handle any of life's difficulties (Matthew 7:13-27). A clear value emerges here, one which intentional adults seeking to empower students must fully embrace and spotlight for their young people. We must teach the Bible as truth to be obeyed, not knowledge to be accumulated. In fact the goal of scriptural knowledge alone may not only be insufficient; it may be detrimental to our spiritual health, as it was for the Pharisees (Matthew 28:20; Mark 7:11-13; Luke 8:11-15, 11:28; John 5:36-40).

Some of us get tripped up by our own education and have come to think of Bible teaching as *presentation*. This approach is often impersonal and content-centered. More importantly, it can cut us off from the real-life, real-time, dynamic application the Holy Spirit wants to customize for each of us. At the other end of the spectrum are those who are infatuated with their stockpile of wisdom and freely steer teens through combinations of peer discussions, movie or music reviews, or their own advice giving. They, too, mismanage the use of God's Word to form courageous hearts and a contagious faith.

Real change and spiritual maturity happen when biblical content confirms, explains, and interprets what we experience as life's reality. Honoring Scripture as the preeminent source of truth is a value we want students to catch throughout their student ministry journey. If our only use of Scripture occurs when we relegate a portion of our meeting times to Bible study, we'll marginalize the importance and relevance of God's Word. Rather, we need to learn how to *conversate* Scripture, naturally drawing it into any discussion we have with young people. We must coach them to obedience by modeling the circulatory function the Bible has in our own lives, as it flows freely between heart, head, and hands. We want to empower teens to infuse their daily lives with meaning and direction by subjecting each experience to the light of God's Word for scrutiny and interpretation by the Holy Spirit.

UNITY

As earlier identified, the love of God breaks down barriers and harmonizes relationships. One important additional truth is that when God's love gathers God's people into otherwise unexplainable communities, the expression of unity actually reveals, or *glorifies*, God in our world (John 17:20-23). The fact that unity itself is a force to be reckoned with has been known since the tower of Babel (Genesis 11:1-9). Nowhere is this power as clearly evidenced as in the days of the early church, when *being together* was a normal precipitator for unleashing the power of God (Acts 1:12-14; 2:1-4, 42-47; 5:12-15). It's safe to say that when we embed the value of unity as a socializing force in our student ministries, our teens will be exposed to an impressive transformational power.

But we could inadvertently settle for less than this important value. Many youth ministries practice what might be called program unity—that is, they seek unity for all of those who choose to participate in the activities of the group.

Though a nice experience for those young people who already belong, there's not much extraordinary about unity if it's possible to define the population as "those who are already predisposed to Christianity and want to hang out with us."

One thing is certain: This sort of programmatic "feel-goodism" falls short of the more radical biblical unity that is the subject of so much admonishment and instruction in letters to the early church. For that unity Paul made clear that party affiliations must be set aside, a collective dwelling of the Holy Spirit was being built, and extraordinary preservation efforts were to be exerted (1 Corinthians 1:13-15; 3:16-17; Ephesians 2:19-22; 4:1-6, 11-16). To the Colossians alone he provided a connecting arc from the supremacy of Christ through the subjection of cultural and ethnic distinctions so that the believers might weave the smallest details of their life together into a unified tapestry that honored the name of God (Colossians 1:15-20; 2:1-3; 3:11-17). John even wrote a small, personal letter to encourage a friend to hold together the coalition in his church dedicated to hospitality and love in spite of the disruptive threat of one person's love for power (3 John).

Far from being a descriptor of internal group health, biblical unity will force most student ministries to get beyond themselves in order to practice oneness with those in their communities who are also part of the body of Christ. That value will require adults to model courageous leadership—exactly the point of being intentional about matters of socialization. The vision of the kingdom of God young people acquire as a result of investing in biblical unity is exciting, compelling, and worthy of sacrifice—a far more empowering and fruitful outcome than might be expected from lesser versions of unity.

CURRICULAR PLANS

We want to be guided by the central vision of empowering students for a courageous and contagious faith. And the hierarchy of formational experiences requires our next priority to be clear minded about the sort of values we want our students to catch from participating with us in ministry. Four were identified and discussed; now they provide additional clarity for curricular planning.

Though educational theorists take a wider view of such things, for our purposes we're narrowly defining *curricula* according to its Latin roots: It's the course to be run in order to accomplish a defined learning goal. Most youth ministers think of curriculum in even more concrete terms, such as purchased material from publishing specialists. This sort of decision making may be an inevitable reality for contemporary ministry. But it doesn't absolve adult leaders from their responsibility to align their curricular plans with established priorities.

It will assist our growth as intentional leaders to reflect on our choices. How does each eight-week lesson series reinforce the transformational values of prayer, love, God's Word, or unity? Does the sum of the semester calendar support the vision of empowering students for a courageous and contagious faith? If we're not vigilant we can make decisions that move us along from month to month, offering students light substance—curricular fiber-fill at best. Such moves are not without consequence; they're now part of the mix of formational experiences for students and may work against our ultimate purposes.

It's also important to recognize the relationship between curricular plans that are built for formal instruction and those that are designed to deliver informal activities and experiences. A goal for both is to help students grow into an understanding of biblical truth. Sometimes teens simply need to learn what the Bible says, for instance, about the love of God and how we are to extend that love to others. Other times the need is to discover what it's like to personally experience God's love through Christian brothers and sisters. But make no mistake—both are critical to the formation of mature, courageous hearts and a faithful, contagious lifestyle.

When it comes to curricular plans, one size does not fit all. Context, history, and student readiness should all be weighed before selecting or designing the routines and courses for learning in a year. But some best practices have emerged from our research observations and subsequent years of discussion with graduate students that may be worth considering when making your plans. See if this curricular framework is helpful to the process of empowering students for courageous and contagious faith:

PHASE I: *Assemble a team of students and adults committed to doing this journey together.*

- Never hurry this process at the expense of making decisions that you may later regret.

- Think of this as a process that starts with open opportunities for orientation, training, and screening experiences that feed into an entry point where a mutual commitment is affirmed.

- Consider the value of creating multiple starting points for orientation, training, and screening, yet maintaining a single, formal point of entry to the team each year.

- Guide the process by the question: "What can/will I do to assemble a team of students committed to being empowered by adults for a courageous and contagious faith?"

- Assess the process by the question: "How can/will I determine that the right team is in place for now?"

Phase II: *Nurture the team focus while they journey together.*

- Our research on student-leader evangelistic effectiveness helps crystallize students' expectations around a clean, triple-threat program focus: *Pray Hard. Invite Often. Explain Well.*

- Youth for Christ's 3Story curriculum reinforces each of the transformational values while offering specific coaching assistance for each program focus.

- Set up weekly structures that allow for adults and students to meet, encourage one another, and be accountable to one another for their heart's integrity and faith's influence.

- Guide this process by the question: "What can/will I do to continually nurture the team's understanding of—and dedication to—being empowered by adults for a courageous and contagious faith?"

- Assess this process by the question: "How can/will I measure the dedication of students to this cause?"

Phase III: *Equip the team for success during the journey together.*

- Empower students and adults alike by soliciting their input before agreeing together on what success looks like for both individual students and the overall team.

- Offer a consistently dependable menu of meetings, retreats, camps, and events students can use as tools to invite those friends with whom they're seeking to share the love of Christ.

- Guide this process by the question: "What can/will I do to foundationally train and responsively coach the team so we can be effective in our common cause?"

- Be sure to appreciate the distinctions between *foundational training*, which can be facilitated through a master curriculum plan like 3Story, and the more dialogical style of *responsive coaching*, which best takes place in the context of a shared life with adult mentors.

- Assess this process by the question: "How can/will I assess student leader effectiveness?"

Continuous Phase: *Organize and care for the adults who support and co-lead the journey.*

- Help adults understand what's expected of them in clear terms. (Our research suggests that adults should 1) *see* students first as Christians whose hearts need to be courageously formed and then as contagious faith leaders among their friends; 2) *be* in weekly accountability settings with either small groups or individual students; and 3) *free* these students to *pray, invite,* and *tell* by offering themselves as available resources to consistently offer appropriate Christian programs, training, and instruction for Christian life.)

- Design, align, and sustain the necessary programs and structures that will be most effective at empowering students for courageous and contagious faith.

PROGRAM FOCUS

If we've been effective at keeping curriculum plans aligned with socialization values and our ultimate purpose, we can increase the likelihood that the programs we focus on will be fruitful in forming students' hearts and lives. Our research has helped us to discern three distinct ways students who are effective at evangelism distinguish themselves from others. They pray harder, invite often, and explain their faith well.

Adults who are intentional program providers will build upon the entire range of formative experiences used to shape such students. The values of prayer, love, God's Word, and unity create a fertile socialization soil for students to naturally and powerfully acquire courageous and contagious traits. Aligned curricular plans ensure that these implicit values are explicitly explored. We are about to look carefully at how praying harder, inviting more often, and explaining well aren't the only results of an empowered student's life. These program concentrations help unleash their potential as leaders of influence among their peers. Each of the next three chapters will give us the chance to focus on that which makes the most difference in empowering students for evangelism among their friends.

But before moving into a concentrated look at these outcome details, let's get fired up by thinking again about what we hope for. There's a lot at stake.

STOKING THE VISION

Veteran youth workers don't have trouble agreeing that natural social pressures characterize the informal world of young people, in which friends wield escalating influence on one another. Students sample their first beer or sexually experiment when their friends support such adventures. More than TV, music, sports, education, and even family, adolescents—at least for a time—tend to lend the influential authority to their closest friendship circle.

This is bad news for those who think funding elaborate institutional programs will bring about lasting change, but it plays wonderfully into how we've come to understand God's transformational processes. Every Christian is called to flavor their particular peer culture as Christ-salt, to be the Jesus light-shafts their friends need. Students who intentionally build bridges of love to their friends will find ever-expanding opportunities to influence in Jesus' name.

We think this explains Troy's high school experience. After putting his faith in Christ as a high school sophomore, he began to work on influencing his friends during his junior year. He seemed to consider each activity he was involved in, each circle of acquaintances, as a chance to reach out. By the time he was a senior, he saw his school routine as a series of strategic evangelism sites. The two-hour chemistry lab at the end of each day afforded him great opportunity to talk about the Lord above the hum of the centrifuge. He hung out with the before-school bench jockeys so he could get a hearing for the gospel. As swim-team manager, he served his team with enough good nature and excellence that he won their respect. His daily job in the student sales booth became a touch point for conversations with kids who were ready to talk about spiritual things. He'd regularly invite folks to church, Campus Life, and Young Life, often packing out his little car when giving rides. By the end of the first semester of his senior year, 18 of his friends had put their faith in Jesus Christ.

If you spend much time hunting for Troy-types—as we have—you'll find his story is more exceptional than normal. Certainly the Lord's timing, gifts, and calling are essential to understanding his case. But we think Troy also stumbled into the kind of strategic pattern for evangelistic mission that our Lord intended to be more common for us Christians. It's most certainly effective among high school students, a population in which the social economy is anything but formal.

Clearly, helping students nurture the faith at the very core of their existence is critical to their ability to fulfill the ends for which they were created. And this faith growth in their hearts is dependent upon their personal knowledge of Jesus Christ. We can't hope to help young people develop Christ-like character, relate to others like Jesus, or be faithful in accomplishing what he wants if their understanding of him is inaccurate...or so abstract that it's disconnected from the complicated realities of their own lives. If our best students are only valued because they *do* evangelism, they will likely not be nurtured in a growing relationship with Jesus Christ.

Our goal is to form courageous hearts with identities hidden, and secure, in Christ.

Our goal is also to form a contagious faith propelled into wide circulation by the love of Christ. Don't we stunt the growth of our Christian teens if we encourage them to cultivate friendships exclusively with one another? Our spiritual maturity is demonstrated by the hunger to copy the Lord as he related to everyone, including those who are lost. According to Ephesians 4, we've got to be about equipping God's teen-people for works of service until all of us are built up to maturity.

Some might wonder if teens can be so equipped. Can they own the responsibility of reaching their friends for Christ and helping them to grow in Christ? The description of our research findings throughout this book ought to help answer cautious folks on this matter. And even though there is ample evidence to affirm that the answers to these two questions are both a resounding yes, some youth workers—like some dysfunctional parents—will have a tough time letting go of their favorite ministry thrill (evangelism). Some of us meet our own needs to have our egos stroked by teens whose dependence on us feeds our own sense of worth. Whatever the motive, our shortsightedness smothers our teens with false love, stunting their spiritual growth and inhibiting their contributions to the important work of God's kingdom.

No one is exempt from the Lord's expectations of us. Jesus calls every member of his body to do their part. We aren't at liberty to lower the bar simply because our own experience suggests it might not be common for teens to step up to this serious task. In fact, we believe our nearsighted vision may contribute to the unnecessary limitations placed upon our teens. Persons rise to uncharted territories of personal accomplishment all the time, boosted by the positive hope and encouragement of those who tell them there's no reason they can't. We believe the Bible supplies both a vision and challenge for students to live up to. Our research has helped us to confirm that youth ministries can actually pull off this faith-informed picture of what teens can accomplish when they're properly equipped to serve the Lord.

Most of us would agree teens are typically in the test-drive stage of their maturity. Judgments are often erratic, decisions impulsive. Raging hormones wield too much influence. Teens don't usually possess the depth of life experience that is so valuable to critical thinking and focused direction.

Yet, in the midst of the gaggle of teens bumping into each other at your local high school are a few that seem to be different. They are nearly steady in the way they live their lives. The existence of these exceptions whispers to us the possibility of a life of courageous dedication to Jesus Christ, daily demonstrated by students who realize that their hope for influence among their friends is wedded to the integrity of their lives.

Let's raise the bar of expectation. We insist that students can take seriously a standard of consistency that results in contagious faith living, welcoming the scrutiny that their spiritually starved peers will place on their lives.

Students can meet the challenge. It's our job to empower them to do so.

CHAPTER FIVE

PROGRAM FOCUS —
PRAYING HARD

The gun sounded and the runners pushed from the metal blocks, bursting with extra power as each began the sprint. The crowd stood as the athletes focused on their goal. All that stood between each runner and the finish line was a series of hurdles, each set to its highest. The runners neared the first hurdle at speed, footsteps in sequence, and jumped forward. One of the slower runners snagged the first hurdle with his trailing foot and crashed to the old cinder track, bouncing three times as he tried to protect himself with his arms.

Cinders, an inexpensive mix of gravel and other sharp objects seemingly designed to punish a body unfortunate enough to fall on it, were once used by schools as a track surface. As I (Terry) stood from my fall, it was apparent that the chore of cleaning the wounds that covered my arms was not going to be pleasant. The scars from that day lasted for years.

If youth leaders and their students lined up to run the race of effective evangelism, they would see a series of hurdles facing them as they pushed out to reach that goal. We discovered in our work that the first hurdle for groups who want to be effective in their witness is prayer. Most of us already know that, and we see it commanded and exemplified repeatedly in Scripture. Nevertheless, to see the direct connection between prayer and fruitful ministry over and over again in our research was remarkable. Seeing others come to Christ is not something adult leaders and students can produce by their will, dynamic leadership, or expert skills. If we see evangelistic effectiveness as something we can produce merely by our programmatic planning, dynamic leadership, or expert skills, then the lack of prayer will be our tripping point. Sometimes the scars from ineffective or insensitive evangelism can last for a long time—for all involved.

ESSENTIAL STEPS

This discussion about the importance of prayer goes right to the heart of what we believe about which of our efforts matter the most. Youth ministry is a mix of fun, dynamic communication, camps and mission trips, planning, outreach events, one-on-one appointments, working with parents, worship music, small groups, large events, vision statements, building relationships, mentoring, laughing together, crying together, and developing lifelong friendships. It's an amazing assortment of finding the lost, leading the found, fixing the hurt, and following Christ.

In the middle of this great mixture often comes the moment of truth as students encounter Christ and his good news, interacting with the Holy Spirit regarding salvation or issues related to healing and obedience. Many youth-ministry ingredients (see the previous list) can be part of leading students to encounter God, but conviction, cleansing, and redemption require God to act. In spite of attempts to understand how we leaders can more effectively help people come to Christ, evangelism is still a supernatural event—an event that God authors.

We can easily fall into the trap of trying to minister strictly on our human strength. The end result may be quite impressive, earning admiration and even applause, perhaps serving as a model to others. However, as Chuck Swindoll warns, "To all who are engaged in ministry, a warning is appropriate. Every project you undertake can be accomplished your way or God's way. The energy source of human strength is impressive, logical, and effective. It works! Initially, folks cannot tell the difference. A ministry built by the energy of the flesh looks just like a ministry built by the energy of the Spirit. Externally, I warn you, it looks the same. But internally, spiritually, down deep in the level of motive, you know in your heart God didn't do it; you did it! There is no glory vertically. And equally tragic, there is no grace horizontally."[27]

> Prayer has to be intentional and at the heart of what the group does. From this central home each element of a youth ministry can house faithfull steps where students and adults expect to see people come to Christ.

There have been many books written on evangelism, and every Christian publishing company has a current title dedicated to the topic. We have read most, each calling the church to greater effectiveness in its witness through example or word. Yet, do a quick review of their chapter titles and you'll find very little on prayer. It's not that the authors don't value it. It's just that most of us assume it happens—and that's an unnoticed hurdle we need to clear.

Prayer must be intentional and at the heart of what the group does. It's part of its mission. Youth ministries that routinely see teens reaching teens for Christ have adopted a God-dependant posture that centers on prayer. From this central home, each element of a youth ministry can house faithful steps where students and adults expect to see people come to Christ.

Jim Cymbala challenged the church to understand that prayer should be central to ministry is his book *Fresh Wind, Fresh Fire*. As he reflected on his transformational ministry, he observed, "The feature that is supposed to distinguish Christian churches, Christian people, and Christian gatherings is the aroma of prayer. It doesn't matter what your tradition or my tradition is.... The Bible does say, 'My house shall be called a house of prayer for all nations.' Preaching, music, the reading of the Word—these things are fine; I believe in and practice all of them. But they must never override prayer as the defining mark of God's dwelling."[28]

Scripture says that we're to continually "seek" the Lord's face (1 Chronicles 16:11) in a continual conversation of inquiry and consultation with him as we allow him to guide our life and ministry. We are to ask (Matthew 7:7; John 16:24), pray so we don't fall into temptation (Matthew 26:41), pray when we feel like giving up (Luke 18:1), and pray when we're in trouble (James 5:13). "Race pace" for one who wants to see others come to Christ is being faithful in prayer (Romans 12:12; Ephesians 6:18; 1 Thessalonians 5:17).

This is a good time to stop and reflect on our own prayerfulness, both individually and corporately with our students. Think through the following questions that have been a challenge to our prayer lives:

- What would your closest friends say about your prayer life? Do they know that you pray? Should they know?

- What is your prayer pattern or prayer frequency? Where did you learn that pattern—culture, family, Scripture, your own weekly schedule?

- If you listed the top three things you pray about each week, what would they be? Where would seeing others come to Christ rank on the list?

It can be a tough challenge to consider whether others would say our lives are marked by prayer. But let's transition to focus on our students—what are their prayer patterns? What do they pray about? To press further, what do *you* pray about *with* them? Research supports the scriptural reality that we need to take prayer seriously and be missional about what we pray for. We need to think strategically about how we pray as a group.

Two developments in the church will assist leaders in their pursuit of leading prayerful change in their ministries. First, the dominance of worship structures in churches today creates a solid footing for incorporating more intentional moments of prayer. Whether in a contemplative worship style or one centered around praise choruses, the challenge will be to help people move from Jesus-and-me thinking to a focus on others and on seeing people come to Christ.

The second helpful step may be a bit surprising, but many who are involved in effective evangelism would report that most non-Christians are interested in talking about God, spirituality, and prayer.[29] In fact, some approaches to evangelism *start* by praying with non-Christians as a first step to talking about spiritual matters.[30]

We need to think strategically about how we pray as a group.

As we've traveled outside of Western culture, we have seen that in places where the church is growing tremendously and with great effect, prayer is a central practice. In fact when Christians gather for a meal or just for coffee, they don't leave the table without praying together—and no "thanks for food" prayers, either. These are apostolic prayers, mini-commissions to go and be salt and light, fruitful in ministry. Very New Testament. Very passionate about seeing people come to Christ. Very empowering.

PRAYER IS THE KEY PRACTICE

The key practice that distinguishes evangelistically fruitful student leaders from others is their patterns of prayer. Examine the lives of student leaders who are effectively reaching others for Christ and you'll find young people who are praying. At the moment a student begins to interact with God for the sake of seeing another come to Christ, a change takes place. Something within these students begins to grow so God can use them to reach their friends for Christ (Ephesians 1:18-19). One of the most concrete and consistent findings in our research solidified this reality. *The more often students prayed for others to come to Christ, the more God used their outreach efforts to help their friends come to Christ.*

Now, not all students in these groups were praying with tremendous frequency. In fact 78 percent of the surveyed students reported they prayed only once a month for opportunities to share their faith. But students whose discipline was to pray weekly for opportunities to share their faith also reported playing a key role in seeing one to three of their friends come to Christ. And for students who prayed even more frequently, a few times a week? Four or more of their friends put their faith in Christ through the influence of these oft-praying friends.

One significant hurdle for students is to pray in groups for others to come to Christ. Group prayer is a cornerstone activity for evangelistically effective teens and youth groups. Some groups from our study cultivated only monthly team-prayer efforts. This occasional effort lessened the impact members of the group had on helping others come to Christ. Such student leaders reported anemic results connected to their witness. On the other hand, when groups reported that they prayed together for lost friends on a weekly basis, God moved through them to help their peers believe in Jesus in pretty remarkable ways.

For a long time a prominent youth pastor watched with restlessness as his "successful" large youth group grew. Something was missing. Students weren't popping with spiritual vibrancy. They lacked excitement when it came to reaching others for Jesus Christ. They weren't evangelistically explosive, and the adult leaders had difficulty figuring out what was wrong. Could it be that their students weren't praying often enough for opportunities to help their friends come to Christ?

We're lost if God doesn't move on our behalf—and not just in a theological sense. We are literally without a clue and helpless to bring about the transformation that must happen in people's lives unless God acts supernaturally.

So why isn't prayer foundational? Do we just assume prayer is happening? It's a strong possibility that too few of us model, facilitate, orchestrate, or coach prayer to the necessary depth. This came as one of the personal challenges we took away from our research. Perhaps we don't establish the prominence and routine of prayer as vital to the lives of adolescents *or* their leaders!

Maybe prayer was once a discipline in our lives, but it has fallen by the wayside as we've grown in our competency and skills. That's my (Dave's) story. My earliest patterns as a new Christian in high school included exchanging prayers with a friend during first period class every day during the first semester of my senior year. This sort of behavior allows one to be very specific when praying, asking God for detailed intervention like supplying an opportunity that very day to talk with a friend who was somewhere along the journey toward trusting Christ as Savior. The number of people who became Christ-followers during this time of life was amazing, clearly making this the most personally fruitful time of my walk with the Lord. I'm not proud to confess that it took this research project to help me understand the link between the frequency and specificity of my prayers for evangelism and my outreach effectiveness.

CREATING SPACE FOR PRAYER

If your desire is to see teens come to Christ, become mature in their love for Jesus, and share him with others, then a consistent prayer life is essential. But our 21st century pace has grown even faster. We're wired by caffeine and achievement, weary from the breakneck pace created by our insatiable desire to squeeze as much as possible out of every moment and dollar. If we come to God at all, we come to him wired and tired.

We try to balance an incredible amount of activities: Working, playing, raising a family, ministering, reading, blogging, watching TV, impressing others, keeping in shape, keeping appointments with accountability partners, staying connected with extended family, answering cell phones, more blogging, paying bills, participating in a small group or two, following our favorite sports teams, watching the latest online video, going to movies, talking about the new whatever we want to buy next—and reporting it all on our blogs. No wonder that in many modern lives, God has little room to exercise his lordship! It's an exhausting pace we keep, even worse for teenage students as they add layers of intensity to the issues of acceptance, family, and academic performance they're already dealing with.

We found youth ministries that help kids to reprioritize life. They've created space for prayer and helped kids wedge it into their lives. Leaders have shifted their focus, their hearts, their schedules, and their mindsets away from "running a youth group," so they can intentionally and proactively cultivate the expectation of experiencing God. Such is the stuff of courageous heart formation.

> Put students in the presence of the Lord for significant periods of time; don't just talk about it.

We detected this new direction in two areas: The focus of the weekly programs and the comments of the youth leaders. Weekly programs were focused on solid biblical teaching and a combination of prayer and worship. When we compiled the original research, we detected a shift from program elements to more prayer and worship. At the same time there was a commitment to excellent biblical teaching, not just experiential and topical meetings. This priority shift became clear when particular youth leaders shared their thoughts with us: "Put students in the presence of the Lord for significant periods of time; don't just talk about it."

THREE PRAYER PRIORITIES

So how come—with all that has been written on prayer (how to do it, how to teach it, and why it's important)—we still struggle with just going for it and seeing what God can do as we rely on the Holy Spirit? Three clear steps emerge from this study as common to those groups in which students had seen their friends become Christians. They are simple behaviors, and as is true of many such uncomplicated truths, the pay-off comes from the discipline of actually doing them. Those youth ministries most effective in helping teens reach teens with the gospel learned that God moved powerfully as they sought him often and openly. See if you can imagine what it would take for your youth ministry to be characterized by these three descriptions.

ADULT LEADERS PUT PRAYER AT THE TOP OF THEIR PRIORITY LIST.

> If we truly want to disciple and develop our students, we'll pray for them, in front of them, alongside them, and give them the opportunity to pray with us, for us, and alongside us.

Prayer starts with modeling. When the disciples asked Jesus to teach them to pray, it was after they'd seen their leader go off by himself to talk with the Heavenly Father (Luke 11:1-13). Chapter 2 highlighted this primary role adults must play in the lives of students who will be effective at reaching their friends for Christ. We must embrace the role of *first models*. We cannot live lives of hollow spirituality, propped up by our impressive and flashy ministry skills. If we truly want to disciple and develop our students, we'll pray for them, in front of them, alongside them, and give them the opportunity to pray with us, for us, and alongside us. If we do it often enough, naturally enough, they'll catch on.

What do you pray for your youth ministry? What does the eighth-grade student pray for? Do your students see and hear your adult leaders pray "real" prayers? This posture of dependency on God must be established as a natural part of our lives. From such times, and *in* such times, we engage *in* the battle for our lost friends. Our students need to know us as people who pray ambitiously and creatively for those without Christ.

STUDENTS MUST PRAY WITH EVER-INCREASING FREQUENCY.

Many times when a group reprioritizes to create an emphasis on prayer, they'll spend a lot of time talking about prayer, teaching on prayer, and showing examples of prayers, but spend little time in actual prayer. As we take students out on the rocky terrain, it's simply not good enough to pray once a month for opportunities to share or to pray even once a week during a group meeting for a friend to come to Christ. Prayer should become a natural part of our existence where we're able to respond appropriately no matter what may come our way.

STUDENTS MUST HAVE OPPORTUNITIES MORE THAN ONCE A MONTH TO PRAY WITH OTHERS.

We adults should facilitate such opportunities. This is a key focus in an old book by Ros Rinker titled *Prayer: Conversing with God.* She asks, "If all this [benefit] and more is waiting for us when we pray with one another and with Him, why is it that so few persons today meet to pray together? We spend hours in time-consuming pleasant conversation. We talk for an hour on the telephone. We all know how to talk. And we talk. Why then do we find so many excuses not to talk with the Lord Jesus, and with each other in His presence?"

Because fear is one of the chief obstacles to cultivating a healthy prayer life (we'll discuss this later), it became painfully clear that its source is our own pride. Rinker observed this as well: "The real basis for not wanting to pray with someone else (aside from not wanting to answer the call of the Good Shepherd and come under His authority and His care) is usually human pride."[31]

Some of us need to get a hold of some change strategies here. As we move our youth ministries from program-centeredness to person-centeredness, we need to be reminded that we have no greater personal need than cultivating a healthy relationship with God. Prayer is central to such a relationship.

One group involved in this study deliberately set out to make this important change. Their process is worth learning from. They focused their energy on expecting God to work in their midst and to use them to reach their friends for Christ. The group stepped away from the need to always play games or try to impress. They stepped away from living in fear of going for it in evangelism. They simply tried to focus on God together. What an adventure!

Youth for Christ's 3Story curriculum embeds this priority in their evangelism training. They teach that the first step in helping friends come to Christ is the move we make toward personally abiding deeper in the life of God—not what we might have traditionally considered outreach steps.[32]

Don't look for a quick fix in the pages describing this research. A ministry that facilitates adults' involvement in teens' lives and emphasizes meeting God in prayer takes a lot of work. Being faithful to truth is worth the effort, even when it challenges other longstanding values or dearly held methods. It can be scary and dangerous to change youth ministry practices, but if we come to God in our inadequacies, admitting our need for his direction and leading, it can be the greatest Christian adventure of all.

FINAL THOUGHTS

There is a danger in prayer, especially when prayer is focused to see others come to Christ. Of course we need to pray for others to come to Christ, but prayer's essential focus must always be God himself, not what we want God to do for us.

We are to be concerned and pray earnestly for the lost, but we've got to be careful to not see prayer as simply another step in getting something done. If we fall into that trap, we'll discover we have changed the very nature of our relationship with God, corrupting it in dangerous ways. Prayer will be exhibit A in the evidence of our self-centered spirituality instead of the evidence of our self-abandonment to God and his purposes.

It's important to weigh the implications of prayer and evangelism. While we are commanded to ask (Matthew 7:7-8; 21:22; John 14:13-14; 1 John 5:14), we're also reminded to "remain" in him (John 15:7) as we ask. Jesus further stated that not everyone who talks to God (Matthew 7:21-23), or even prophesies, will enter the kingdom of heaven. Rather, the final measure is based on whether God really knows us. In the midst of our emphasis on prayer for the purpose of evangelism, we dare not forget prayer's non-negotiable priority: Friendship with God.

> Prayer's essential focus must always be God himself, not what we want God to do for us.

While talking with youth groups participating in our research project, we commonly asked if they would like to tell us anything important about themselves that they feared might be missed by our data-collection methods. In one group a young man jumped on the opportunity, quickly declaring "Prayer is big." It sure is. It's the Possibility Step, the one that allows God to move in our midst. When God moves to bring about evangelistic fruitfulness, the excitement is tough to contain. Student leaders experience life-changing evidence of God's activity in their lives, a reference point that can never be erased.

They'll never be the same.

CHAPTER SIX
PROGRAM FOCUS — INVITING OFTEN

Troll through the middle or high school in any community and you'll spot young people who belong to a student ministry group. They're trying to make it through the many activities that vie for their time and attention, just like every other student. Stop and listen to their daily concerns and you'll quickly discover the social forces that fashion the daily dynamics of their activities. This relational give and take of mutual influence (what some call "peer pressure") creates an invisible undertow to the regular schedules of any school. These forces push and produce waves of influence while students choose to ride a particular fad or participate in certain activities. The social undertow can explain certain hairstyles, clothing options, peer group choices, or risky behaviors that some kids make.

This is why good research is helpful to those of us working with youth. We can dive past the surface, where we often make observations shaped by our own history and perspectives, to see the social meanings that lie beneath. Once we collect data and stories, we can remap the environment from this more detailed perspective. We have the ability to focus on and learn from particular students of influence who navigate the daily dynamics and play key roles in seeing their friends come to Christ.

Parents often get to glimpse the social world of the local school and neighborhood through their own teens' eyes. It's interesting to watch adolescents choose where and with whom to spend their time. When invited to a home or activity, kids often work through a mental checklist of the characteristics of that home to see if it's a place they want to go. If you reflect back to your own childhood, was there one house where you and your friends used to spend most of your time? Chances are it was particularly inviting, and all the kids wanted to go there...but it took an invitation. Or maybe there was a special party with the invite list that determined who was in and who was out in a particular class or school. If a kid wasn't invited, they could feel undesired and left out. It's tough for parents to navigate how to provide support, even though most of us have gone through the ordeal ourselves.

The social checklist is a common way to think through shared opportunities. Will they be awkward in any way? Will I be embarrassed? Who else will be there? Will there be good food? Will there be fun stuff to do—sports, video games, movies, etc.? We not only have to be invited, but the nature of the event and the warmth and acceptance of the people are interwoven within the inviting words.

In a consumeristic culture, we constantly steer through invitations from companies to purchase or participate in the latest and greatest. Hotels show us their comfortable beds and available swimming pools, and coffee or pastry shops let the smells do an effective sales job. What made the best wedding invitation that you ever received so striking? Have you ever been somewhere, unaware that you're hungry, until the smell of sizzling steak or a Chinese food buffet grabs your attention? How did you feel when you first walked into the church that you call your home church? When did you know that you truly belonged somewhere?

It's a problem when some think it's *only* the community that witnesses—that the *only* thing the individual must do is invite. They don't recognize their role in creating a consistently credible and welcoming atmosphere. But students who reach others for Christ understand the connection between the community dynamics of their youth group as a witness and their verbal invitations to others. By engaging in the act of inviting their friends, they bridge that wrongly perceived gap.

Much of the current literature about evangelism emphasizes the important role of the community—that people often belong to a group (attending its group meetings) before they believe. Though this may usually be true, there is a subtle danger if we ignore what we've learned about the role of verbal invitation in outreach. Evangelistically effective students demonstrate courageous hearts through a Christian lifestyle and combine that example with verbal invitations to attend a youth group gathering and talk to others about Jesus. Other than Christian parents, this combination of nonverbal and verbal witness by friends is the most significant predictor of teens coming to Christ.

What's distinctive about a student who is effective at reaching his or her friends for Christ? What are the actual differences between a young person who has impacted her peers for Christ and a Christian teen who hasn't? Those teens who are most effective in peer-to-peer evangelism don't necessarily read the Bible any more or any less than other student leaders. They attend church activities with the same regularity as those who have never led others to Christ and often hang out with church friends like every other student. They *are* different because they more frequently invite others to youth group meetings. In fact, our research revealed that inviting is one of the two distinctive roles that our sample of quality student leaders perceived was necessary to doing their job. The more frequently student leaders engaged in inviting behaviors, the more likely they would be to help a greater number of their friends come to Christ. For example, those students who could identify eight or more of their friends having come to Christ invited others to large group meetings a few times a week, while those who couldn't identify a friend becoming a Christian engaged in this kind of inviting activity less than monthly.

There is a direct relationship between students inviting others and their effectiveness at helping lead friends to faith in Jesus Christ. Don't miss the significance of inviting. More than simply helping to build youth group numbers, inviting behaviors can be directly linked to student conversions! Sometimes youth ministries tend to have either an "if we build the program, they will come" philosophy or an "if I say it from upfront, then students will understand it" approach to teaching. This misses the heart of personal invitation, an invitation that invites others into a community of relationships where the gospel is intentionally demonstrated and communicated.

THE HEART OF PERSONAL INVITATION

The heart of invitation is found in God as he initiates his relationship with us all. He invites all to respond to his love: "Come, all you who are thirsty, come to the waters; and you who have no money, come, buy and eat!" (Isaiah 55:1). This divine call in the Old Testament invitation was restated by Jesus: "Let anyone who is thirsty come to me and drink" (John 7:37b). It also serves as the final scene in Scripture as the apostle John writes, "The Spirit and the bride say, 'Come!' And let those who hear say, 'Come!' Let those who are thirsty come; and let all who wish take the free gift of the water of life" (Revelation 22:17). We need to view the act of inviting not as a programmatic function, but as an essential component of evangelistic faithfulness.

Consider how inviting Jesus was in the early stages of his ministry. (For example, see John 1:39-51.) He intimately invited his followers to trust him: "Come to me, all you who are weary and burdened, and I will give you rest" (Matthew 11:28). Jesus' teaching from the parable of the great banquet is about the expanded generosity of a man's invitations in the face of others' excuses (Luke 14:15-24).

Webster's defines *invite* as "to request the presence or the participation of." What a great way to think of it! We desire to have another's presence and their participation with us—not just to add a number to the attendance total, to gain their money for the trip fund, or even to tally a personal decision to follow God—we want *the person*. It's a relational process first—at least it should be.

The apostle Paul showed how this relational focus is at the heart of invitation. The goal of inviting is that all will be reconciled in relationship to God (2 Corinthians 5:11-21). His ministry was built on relationships and on the persuasion of others to follow Christ. He exhorts us to be inviters, "We are therefore Christ's ambassadors, as though God were making his appeal through us. We implore you on Christ's behalf: Be reconciled to God" (2 Corinthians 5:20).

At this intersection of verbal invitation and the evidence of community is a very scriptural idea that doesn't get much traffic in church circles today. What does it mean to exercise hospitality? In biblical times, it meant to welcome the traveler by opening one's home to another. The Greek word actually means *loving strangers* and was to be a characteristic of those who desired to be ministers (I Timothy 3:2; Titus 1:8). It was to be a common practice among Christians (Romans 12:13; Hebrews 13:2), to be exercised without grumbling (1 Peter 4:9).

If we consider that loving strangers was an integral part of the New Testament church and a required characteristic for church leaders, its absence in today's churches is worth reflection. What does *welcoming strangers* look like in today's culture? When was the last time your church, your student ministry, you and your family, or others in your church exemplified the welcoming of strangers? Perhaps the answers may explain why we don't hear much today about this early church practice. Youth ministries who have evangelism as part of their communal vision know and practice how to welcome new students well.

The heart of personal invitation beats from a God who invites all to be in relationship with himself. His message is entrusted to praying people and communities who should contagiously model what it looks like to be a Christ-follower. When combined with courageous verbal invitations, the potential for seeing people take notice and want to dive in is significant. They truly can become "inviting" communities.

AN INVITING COMMUNITY

When we first set out to research effective evangelistic groups, we expected to discover some super-evangelist students, like those you hear about at youth worker conferences. You know—the ones witnessing to others at the local Taco Bell on a Friday night, or the dynamic student leader who single-handedly leads Bible study groups of over 100 students while leaping over tall buildings. There are students who have realized these kinds of ministries for short periods of time, but our search revealed that these intense experiences were short-lived, often attributed to uncommon movements of the Holy Spirit. And they also tend to dissipate once a dynamic senior graduates.

We did find a few students (about 4 percent of our sample) who were so accomplished as evangelists that they played a key role in more than 10 of their friends coming to Christ! However, none of them worked apart from a youth ministry community. Instead they were empowered by an existing youth ministry that fostered their contagious faith, a ministry led by a youth worker committed to evangelism as a key focus for the youth ministry. *These were ordinary teens organized for an extraordinary task, committed to living in ways that would allow God to use them in any way possible to reach their friends.*

So if community plays a key role in the inviting process, then what dynamics of the role of a community showed up in the research? First, let's qualify what types of group experiences are best suited for particular purposes.

Large groups are more "inviting" than small groups. Whatever the inherent flaws or dangers may be in using large groups for youth ministry, these settings provide one of the easiest and most helpful tools for motivated student leaders who want assistance in reaching their friends for Christ. Students invited others to attend large-group meetings more frequently than students who were involved in a small-group format because a person could attend or belong without feeling put on the spot.

That's why the student leaders in our research perceived large-group gatherings to be evangelism-friendly and safer for hesitant friends. They were more likely to issue frequent invitations to non-Christians, could observe teens and adults leading others to Christ more often, and would intentionally build relationships with nonbelievers more often. Large group settings were more helpful than small group settings for students wanting to reach their friends with the gospel.

Both of us are strong proponents of small groups in youth ministry, and we have been longtime participants in them as adults. Some important activities happen when small groups are formed to advance the evangelistic purposes of youth ministry. The work of prayer, already highlighted as critical to the evangelism process, clearly is best facilitated through small groups. Students pray with others for friends to come to Christ, and small groups help people learn how to organize others for prayer. Smaller settings also provided opportunities for a more personal style of evangelism, infrequent though they may be. Adult accountability—also a critical factor contributing to student leader effectiveness—was most clearly evidenced in small groups, and students also could grow into greater degrees of confidence in their personal ministry.

As we traveled coast to coast to meet with these evangelistic youth ministries, students routinely identified four *group* dynamics as important factors to their success. Note that these are group dynamics and relate to both large and small group formats. It's safe to say that if these four components are evident in group settings, there is a greater likelihood your students will invite others with more confidence and frequency.

YOUTH MINISTRY NEEDS TO BE SOCIALLY SAFE.

The most evangelistically effective youth groups demonstrated an understanding of both the social context of their region, city, or school, but also the social dynamics within their group. This keen awareness extended to the design of their meetings and events, careful to not create programmatic moments that would make students (including those who attended regularly) feel socially awkward.

Chances are, most readers can relate to the kind of awkward moments we're talking about. They take a variety of shapes, but effective youth ministries are attuned to how they can be avoided. For example, it's not uncommon for some of the rural and suburban youth ministries around Fort Wayne, Indiana, to enjoy a fall tradition called Egg 'n Beg. It's a simple fundraiser for groups and usually results in kids getting messy with smashed eggs. Those student groups from within the city found that there was no appeal in this activity among their young people whose idea of fun did not include getting their nice clothes trashed by egg yolks. Some well-meaning leaders would have tried to talk their kids into trying something new, but doing so would fail to respect the need for teens to feel socially safe *as they define it*. Transformational youth ministries have found a way to be true to the gospel and yet demonstrate an awareness of adolescent learning styles, social dynamics, and developing values. Youth ministers who spend time with their students in informal settings can learn much of what's needed to ensure this safety by just inquiring and listening. These times are treasures of ministry because they not only build relationships with students, they also provide feedback about how well the youth ministry relates to the important social values of its teens. Students think a lot about whether group meetings will cost them socially. Youth workers need to operate with this mindset, too.

Youth workers often answered our questions about their ministries' success by offering spiritual or structural perspectives. But it was not uncommon for students to answer the same questions using an entirely social orientation. Since one of the main tasks of the student leaders was to invite others, their friends' opinions toward the youth ministry were extremely important. Don't underestimate the pull and power of community to your evangelistic effectiveness. Poor social dynamics of any community can offset the potential in its teaching and other ministry elements.

Student leaders were confident they could invite their friends because their groups had given them confidence that they were socially safe. One student summed it up: "I knew I could invite friends because I felt comfortable there." Another added, "Everyone mobbed us and welcomed us. Instead of being pushed away, I was drawn in." We can't overstress this factor's contribution in the success of students who reach their peers for Christ. *This atmosphere of safety is so important to teenagers that it could enable or disable a youth ministry's outreach to nonbelievers.*

YOUTH MINISTRY NEEDS TO BE EMOTIONALLY SAFE.

Not only did the youth ministries in our research demonstrate understanding of the need for social safety, they also took steps to ensure an emotional safe-zone. Social relevance was never established at the cost of authenticity. Kids were free to be content, sad, hurt, ecstatic, in conflict, and even fragile. Emotional safety demands a level of authenticity that is often difficult to achieve. One group critiqued themselves and realized they were falling short in this area: "We invite [others to events] and hug, but only when people are hurting. We need to care for each other all the time." However, this type of attention to the emotional qualities within each group was common among the groups where teens were reaching teens for Christ. Fortunately, student ministries often get this right when compared to other age-level ministries.

We often see a lack of emotional safety in middle school ministries where adult leaders seem to forget what it was like to be a middle schooler. The energy and enthusiasm that these young teens bring into large group meetings can lull leaders into an inaccurate perception of how important this need is. So while they will laugh together at most anything, when one of the group is on the finger-pointing end of that laughter, the derision is anything but emotionally safe. I (Terry) had such an experience during a youth group stunt resulting in water being poured into the crotch of my pants. I can testify that the smile I braved on the outside did not match the humiliation I felt inside, and I stayed away from that group for quite a while as a result. The issue of readiness we discussed in Chapter 3 is significant to effective leadership with ever-changing adolescents. The ups and downs of teenage life are abrupt, and we need to allow space for emotions without sacrificing or sabotaging the social safety of the community.

YOUTH MINISTRY NEEDS TO EXHIBIT A HIGH LEVEL OF CONSISTENCY.

Students who invite others will do so as long as there are dependable characteristics to the ongoing ministry. Students who were trying to reach their friends wanted to be confident that meetings would be dependable in quality and style, not awkward or surprising. They wanted enough consistency and familiarity in meetings that they could invite friends and know they wouldn't be embarrassed.

Imagine what would happen if there was inconsistency. A student might invite a friend thinking it was going to be a Bible study like last week, and instead finds a battle of the classes competition designed for underclassmen. Worse yet, what if the ministry purposes might change from semester to semester as the latest book or convention shaped the thinking of the youth worker? It's not difficult to see why consistency is an important asset to provide student leaders' confidence to invite others to youth ministry meetings.

YOUTH MINISTRY SHOULD CENTER ON CHRIST.

One of our research team members returned from spending considerable time checking out a well-known youth ministry. She was unimpressed. "If it wasn't for the opening prayer, I couldn't tell that it was a Christian group," she said. No other aspect of that night would have told the uninformed that it was a Christian group. And we've discovered that this is more common than one might expect. We each have listened to youth talks that offered no way of knowing they had anything to do with following Jesus except for a Bible verse added at the end. Too many talks end up coaching kids to act like good people rather than teaching who God is and sharing his invitation to follow him in faithfulness toward maturity. On the other hand, we've witnessed heavy-handed talks that shamed the audience and resembled little of the warmth and personal approach Christ modeled (Matthew 11:28).

Hopefully social and emotional safety and a Christ-centered focus aren't perceived as polar ends of a spectrum, incapable of coexisting together. Those groups realizing peer evangelistic success managed to be distinctly Christian in nature while maintaining a commitment to social relevance. This was integral to the success of their student leaders' inviting practices. The community needs to be socially in step, living out and talking about its Christ-centered identity. Doing so allows others to see what you mean when group members talk about and live out their faith in Christ. Author Brad Kallenberg notes that the gospel often isn't believed on its own—people have to see it in action. "Only against a backdrop of a concrete community that resembles Christ, albeit imperfectly, can the gospel be heard most clearly," he wrote.[33]

Pioneering pastor Alan Hirsch has reemphasized this key element when he discusses missional effectiveness: "For authentic missional Christianity, Jesus the Messiah plays an *absolutely* central role. Our identity as a movement, as well as our destiny as a people, is inextricably linked to Jesus—the Second Person of the Trinity. In fact, our connection to God is only through the Mediator—Jesus is 'the Way'; no one comes to the Father except through Him (John 14:6). This is what makes us distinctly *Christ*-ian."[34]

It's important to not make any of these four factors of healthy groups legalistic. If that happens, then we lose the heart of our ministry. Don't lose the main point here: The research showed that student leaders' *confidence* in the nature of the community to which they invite their friends is the significant finding. Do the students have confidence in the social and emotional safety of the group—that it will be consistent in style and purpose, and that, as they invite their friends, it will be a place with Christ at its center? Paying attention to these areas will aid the efforts of students as they reach out to their friends.

INVITING RELATIONSHIPS

Inviting friends to ministry-related functions is *not* a natural occurrence in a teen's daily relationships. Students naturally embrace being an example to others, an encourager to those in need. However, the students of these evangelistically effective groups saw inviting others to youth group activities as a task to accomplish, sort of like a homework assignment from their youth leader. It's not uncommon to observe Christian students building relationships with non-Christians without ever thinking of inviting them to youth group, telling them what Jesus means to them, or praying for them unless prompted. When youth leaders remind teens about inviting others, it helps them to move past the main obstacles to effective outreach (fear, busy schedule, guilt, and laziness). They begin to see themselves as critical players necessary to reach others for Jesus Christ.

This hesitancy by students to invite friends may be a surprising revelation to youth workers, but it rings true with research done by Huntington University's Link Institute on behalf of Youth for Christ's (and now Youth Specialties') DCLA conferences. Let's see if we can explain the dynamic at work. Imagine Geoffrey, a Christian high school student who spends a considerable amount of time with his unbelieving friends. They might eat together every day in the school cafeteria, talk or text on their cell phones a few times a week, even run on the track team and practice together after school every day. Curious though it may be, Geoffrey doesn't *naturally* invite his friends to youth group. Unless it becomes a conscious thought along the lines of *It's my job to invite them to youth group... here I go,* he likely would not follow through on this task related to reaching his friends for Christ.

Many youth workers have assumed they know the problem when they frame their question, "Why aren't students building relationships with non-Christians so they can invite them?" If we zoom back into the school to watch Geoffrey in action, we would see that he's already surrounded by relationships with non-Christian friends. The task of building relationships for the purpose of evangelism isn't necessary because those relationships are already present. Consider all the daily relational settings that are a part of his world. He sits in each of his classes with various groups of classmates, walks in the halls between classes with his closer friends, sits at the lunch table with a different group of friends, and plays sports with an even different group of friends. In the social framework of the school and his everyday life, Geoffrey and other Christian students don't have to work at building bridges to nonbelievers; those relationships already exist.

Our role as adults is to help nudge, coach, remind, and cajole Christian students to first pray for their friends and then be deliberate in inviting them to meetings or telling them about Jesus. Close your eyes and picture 100 student leaders, each of whom already has relationships with non-Christians. That's the reality. Now ask those to step forward who pray at least weekly for their friends to come to know Christ. The crowd will reduce in size a bit (from our research, about 87 percent would step out), but those who've emerged are likely going to be those who can report reaching at least one of their friends for Christ.

From this smaller group, ask those who are strategic and deliberate in inviting their friends to events where they'll hear the gospel to raise their hand. Most, but not all, hands will go up. This smaller group will be even more evangelistically fruitful than those without their hands in the air. Can you see how this is a crucial turning point contributing to evangelistic effectiveness? (By the way, that group will dwindle a little more when we ask all those who actually tell their friends about their own faith in Christ to take another step forward.)

Students (and parents) might get a bit anxious when a youth ministry begins to emphasize inviting others. Many burned-out groups and leaders tried to pull off a big event only to be disappointed. As always there needs to be a sensitive balance. But inviting also needs to be rooted in a disciple-making focus, as we discussed in earlier chapters. As these groups become communities of hospitality where Christ is central, the group will be inviting to others. However, expecting student leaders to invite others isn't optional if we want students who are routinely seeing their friends come to Christ.

When we dove deeper into the social and spiritual dynamic of invitation, we discovered three specific destinations to which the best student leaders invited their friends. Invitation, we discovered, was more than a programmatic function; it was part of the ministry that these student leaders exercised with their friends. It was still intentional and not natural, but it focused students on the goal of seeing friends come to Christ.

THEY REGULARLY INVITE AND BRING OTHERS TO THE GROUP.

If never prompted to invite more frequently, Christian students in our study invited a friend about once a month to their youth group. Not much usually came of this invitation. On the other hand, those students who played a key role in helping friends come to Christ invited their friends to a group meeting once a week. Even more noteworthy, those students who were most successful in peer-to-peer evangelism invited friends on an almost daily basis.

The act of inviting alone is only part of this overall process. When we interviewed student leaders and asked why they invited their friends, the responses were insightful: "Lots of kids have been saved here." "I became a Christian at this youth group." "I knew the message would be good." "I knew they wouldn't seem nerdy if they opened up." "The leaders devote a lot of attention to us."

Kallenberg captures nicely what happens in these moments, "Because a story line is lived out by the community of Christ-followers, the new convert's identity is necessarily social; one cannot identify oneself as a Christ-follower and avoid identifying oneself with the believing community that is seeking to embody the gospel both in its words and in its life together."[35]

The meetings facilitated an atmosphere where invitations could be bolstered by an evangelistic ministry that students could be proud of. Within the ongoing plans and monthly schedule, careful attention had been given to helping students invite others and providing meetings that were shaped in some way to minister to new students. Rich in biblical truth, effective discipleship, and life-changing teaching, these youth ministries still allowed room for new people to come, be involved on a regular basis, and belong. In fact, they counted on it happening.

THEY INVITE OTHERS TO COME AND TALK WITH CHRISTIAN ADULT YOUTH WORKERS.

As student leaders moved through personal barriers to reach out to others and talked with their friends about Christ, they often desired to involve a Christian adult for help or support. This step was a significant move for student leaders. Nearly 77 percent of the student leaders in our research said they never or seldom invited a non-Christian friend to talk to an adult. But those students who invited friends to talk to a Christian adult on a weekly basis saw more friends come to Christ because of their partnership approach to ministry.

One advantage (previously discussed in Chapter 2) to this teamwork between students and adults is it enables the Christian student to watch evangelism in action. One student research participant from a parachurch ministry commented, "If I could see a gradual process of evangelism, it would be encouraging." This senior girl added, "My friends don't want anything to do with Christ and don't see the need. I don't know how to reach them." She was feeling the need for adult support to grow in her ability to reach those whom she cared about. To reiterate, making adults available as resources for communicating the gospel is crucial to developing evangelistically effective student leaders.

THEY INVITE OTHERS TO HEAR WHAT JESUS MEANS TO THEM.

A third invitation students offer to non-Christian friends is to ask to talk personally about what Jesus means to them. Before the telling of the gospel can actually happen, an invitation to talk usually takes place. We will cover this more completely in the next chapter, but it makes sense that those who have success sharing their faith also regularly practice the discipline of asking others if they want to talk about Jesus. For now, it's important to see how seamless the relationship is between the three elements of evangelistic effectiveness.

ASSESSING YOUR INVITATIONS

One of the benefits of doing substantial research over many years is that we can hear common themes that connect every story and situation and scream for attention. As we listened to hundreds of students and sifted through a variety of research, it was apparent that these young people had reached two significant milestones. First, they had changed their heart focus. (Such feedback has fortified our convictions about forming courageous hearts as a first priority.) These effective youth groups loved their youth for who they were. They revealed a change from an "us-orientation" to a focus on others. They considered their attention to outreach to be an integral part of their youth group. Far more than just a youth worker's hot button, this outlook was embraced by the whole youth ministry and its student leaders.

The second milestone was their adoption of a common mission and goal. They had collectively moved past the usual barriers toward outreach and into the cooperative mission of reaching their friends for Christ. Often accompanied by rallying slogans (like "Be bold!" or "Get out of your comfort zone!" and "Teachers don't make seating charts, God does!"), they constantly reminded each other of the task before them to be people who help bring others to faith in Jesus Christ.

If you're intentional about seeing students come to Christ, then you'll want to reflect on this chapter and consider how well (and often) your student leaders invite their non-Christian friends into settings where they can be exposed to the hope of Jesus. Are adults readily available as resources for evangelistic conversations? Do your meetings and other gatherings reflect the presence of Christ in their content and atmosphere? You may want to talk it over with your students to see how confident they are in the program as they risk inviting their friends. How can you creatively assist your leadership students as they take the initiative to invite their peers?

> Everything in the world is about to be wrapped up, so take nothing for granted. Stay wide-awake in prayer. Most of all, love each other as if your life depended on it. Love makes up for practically anything. Be quick to give a meal to the hungry, a bed to the homeless—cheerfully. Be generous with the different things God gave you, passing them around so all get in on it: if words, let it be God's words; if help, let it be God's hearty help. That way, God's bright presence will be evident in everything through Jesus, and he'll get all the credit as the One mighty in everything—encores to the end of time. Oh, yes! (1 Peter 4:7-11 The Message)

CHAPTER SEVEN

PROGRAM FOCUS — EXPLAINING WELL

School fundraising projects. Ask anyone who's had to lug crocks of cheese, frozen pizzas, discount cards, or boxes of greeting cards to fund a program, and you'll get a variety of negative reactions. Even if the incentive for selling the most barbecue chicken tickets is a flat-screen TV, asking people to buy sausage, Christmas ornaments, or car wash passes is anything but fun. Our history with telemarketers has shaped how we respond to sales efforts.

And it has shaped how we think about verbally sharing the good news of Jesus Christ.

If we can develop a true heart for evangelism, then we can avoid sales-pitch insensitivities, reliance on programs, judgmental proclamations, or the temptation to hide and just let our actions do the talking. We need to be ready to explain the reason for our hope (1 Peter 3:15). We have to be able to let others know how it works to be a Christ-follower. Actions and community alone rarely point others to Christ without accompanying language. A contagious faith is often explained by winsome words.

Review the many books on evangelism and you'll quickly discern what the authors think about sharing their faith with others. You can sense that some were part of a ministry where verbal evangelism was repeatedly championed—and they reacted against that, as if they were being handed a fundraising sales sheet of overpriced items. Yet listen to these collective authors' perspectives and it becomes clear that more people are prepared—and interested—to talk about spiritual matters than ever in recent history. Despite what we think about postmodern influences, we live in a culture where many profess a belief in God, though that belief doesn't directly affect their actions or church attendance. North America has now become the largest English-speaking mission field in the world.[36] People want to talk about spiritual matters—and those who don't attend church are perhaps more comfortable doing so than those who regularly attend church.

Youth ministries that want to see teens help teens come to Christ work diligently to prepare their student leaders to explain the good news well.

IT'S GOOD NEWS

The training of students to be a verbal witness is sometimes lost amidst emphases on Christian discipleship and nurture, but verbal witnessing is the central method God has chosen to spread the good news of Jesus Christ (2 Corinthians 5:11-21). Jesus called the disciples to follow him, promising to change their focus from mere fishing to "fishing" for people (Mark 1:17). The apostle Paul even wrote, "Woe to me if I do not preach the gospel," showing his desire "to win as many as possible" (1 Corinthians 9:16b, 19). The disciples experienced life-changing time with Jesus; it's no wonder they couldn't keep from telling others about Jesus' grace and forgiveness—even in the face of persecution and impending death.

Pastor and author Mark Dever wonders if we can get that same sense of what the gospel is today. "Isn't it amazing that we have trouble sharing such wonderful news? Who would mind telling a friend that they held a winning lottery ticket?

What doctor wouldn't want to tell their patient [about good results]?...So why is it, when we have the best news in the world, that we are so slow to tell it to others?"[37]

Should we expect every kid to become adept at sharing his or her faith? Even in youth groups where teens regularly reach other teens for Christ, sharing the good news wasn't natural for students. When asked how often they explained to friends how to begin a relationship with Jesus, nearly half the students participating in our study said never or seldom. Remember: This response was from student leadership groups with a track record of evangelistic success! Another third claimed they shared the gospel with friends roughly once a month. Clearly the burden of telling in these effective youth groups was carried by the slightly less than 29 percent of students, who reported that they were verbally witnessing more than once a month.

Robert E. Coleman writes about Jesus' objective in the classic book *The Master Plan of Evangelism*, "The days of His flesh were but the unfolding in time of the plan of God from the beginning. It was always before His mind. He intended to save out of the world a people for Himself and to build a church of the Spirit which would never perish."[38] Today's student leaders are key players in this master plan from the heart of the Lord Jesus.

When students take a bold, even rare step to actually share the gospel, supernatural things can happen. If a student tells others about Jesus, our research shows that they've likely been praying regularly, reading their Bible almost daily, and memorizing Scripture to help their efforts.

Sometimes the role of research is to dispel myths created by reputations. When we searched out youth ministries with a strong reputation for peer-to-peer evangelism, we imagined that two-thirds of the students were regularly active in sharing their faith. So when half the student leaders in our study reported that they seldom share the gospel, we became instantly curious. Do their fears play such a big role that they keep students from sharing? Is this inhibition to tell others of Jesus just a natural byproduct of the maturation process? If that's the case, we should be able to see from our research that older students share more frequently than younger students do. Is it even realistic to expect that a majority of our students will tell their friends how to come to a saving relationship with Jesus Christ?

The Typical Student Leader

What profile emerges from our research to describe the typical student leader from these atypical student ministries? Let's look at some clear findings. The typical student leader—

- Has played a key role in one to three friends coming to Christ.

- Has most likely been led to Christ by a parent or key family member.

- Reads the Bible a few times weekly, but not quite daily.

- Thinks the most important thing to do as a leader is to encourage others.

- Cites fear and being too busy as the biggest obstacles to overcome in reaching their friends for Christ.

- Identifies youth workers and friends as their biggest helps in reaching friends for Christ.

- Invites his or her friends to youth group a little more than once a month.

As central as telling is to reaching others for Christ in these reputable ministries, these typical students clearly aren't wild-eyed evangelists.

REGULAR TRAINING

Part of the reason student leaders moved forward in their ministry development was because training in evangelism took place frequently. Effective evangelistic youth groups carry out regular training efforts—be they formal or informal in nature—to help students learn how to become a verbal witness. Even if student leaders have been active only in the first two steps (praying and inviting), there is still the strong possibility that they will find a chance to verbally share with a friend. The training efforts focused on the need to be ready, to know what to say and how to say it. The groups in our study wanted their students to know how to tell others about Jesus. As a common value they also regularly promoted the need to be ready to tell.

So how often is regular? What kind of priority should be placed on evangelism within a youth ministry? How often in the schedule of a youth ministry should youth workers teach student leaders how to share their faith? Can we put too much emphasis on evangelism? We certainly agree that there are ministries whose strong commitment to outreach is practiced in unhealthy, unbalanced ways. In fact, given that each of the groups in our study had excellent ministry reputations, we were surprised by how *much* emphasis these groups put on evangelism. It reminds us that balance doesn't necessarily result in an equal division of time or energy. We believe the deliberate evangelism concentration we found among the groups in our study contributed to the result of teens reaching teens for Christ.

There was a real difference in the practices of student leaders who were coached more than once a month how to share their faith. This was one of the most significant "humps" in the statistical returns from the research. If evangelistic training took place even monthly, then the impact on the evangelistic efforts of students was average or minimal. However, if the frequency of that coaching was increased to more than once a month, there was a notable increase in how many students came to Christ because of their witness. This more-than-once-a-month coaching was accomplished through a combination of focused discussions (at student leader meetings), regular youth group training (another night of the week), and adult mentoring with evangelism as a point of interaction. Taken together—and accompanied by the modeling power of witnessing adults—these supplied a constant rhythm of reminders and instruction about verbal evangelism.

WHAT'S THE MODEL?

Modeling evangelism is one of the best ways to train others how to share their faith. Most, if not all, of the student-leader groups we've observed reflect the personality of the youth leader. The teens often take on their leader's personality, behaviors, values, and even their sense of humor! Students emulate what they see in the life of their leader. So if the adult leaders are convinced of the importance of sharing their faith, it will show up in their student leaders' lives as well.

One youth pastor took his students along with him on evangelistic appointments with his peers. His hope was that they would learn even more about witnessing when they saw *his* nervousness and strategy as he did his own peer-to-peer evangelism. He wasn't just living a life of outreach with teens so his youth ministry would evangelize; he was presenting the gospel to his friends and wanted his teens to catch his passion for reaching lost friends.

There is a very significant point to be pressed here. Some ministries have considered evangelism to be a set of trainable skills. We're convinced evangelism is at least as much a value as it is a combination of trainable abilities. So while skills might be learned through demonstration and talks, values need to be modeled if they will be picked up. That's why it's true that more is caught than taught with regard to equipping students for evangelism.

Students reported that their youth leaders, other student leaders, the youth program, and training times were all most helpful to them as they learned evangelism. A noticeable absence from this list was parents. The parents of students in our research hadn't modeled evangelism well to their children. More than 80 percent of the student leaders said they had never, or seldom, seen their parent lead someone to Christ. In fact, parental influence was a nonfactor in our overall findings—except at the students' original moment of conversion, which usually took place in childhood.

What happened from childhood on the way to adolescence? Only 3 percent of the students identified their parents when asked to describe what was most helpful in their peer-evangelism efforts. Youth leaders were asking their students to engage in a Christian discipline (witnessing) that they had not grown up observing as a value in their parents' lives, though most of these student leaders grew up in Christian homes. This outreach mentality and lifestyle was something they were being introduced to for the first time as they entered a youth ministry. An important logical progression can be observed here. If most persons who come to Christ do so by the age of 18, it may be that their best hope to becoming evangelistic adults is through the experience of a student ministry in their high school or college years.

Given the responsibility to train students how to share, the scriptural importance of our role as God's evangelistic "ambassadors" (2 Corinthians 5:20), and the success of modeling as a training method, youth workers need to deliberately design ways for students to "catch" evangelism from others. Longtime professors of Christian education and formation, Klaus Issler and Ron Habermas describe two forms of modeling: Structured and spontaneous. Structured modeling provides "a regular standard for emulation" and takes the form of classroom features like lectures, dramatic scenes, movies, role-plays, and moments where purposeful demonstration was orchestrated. "Spontaneous modeling is not planned—it just happens," Issler and Habermas write in *How We Learn*. "It is characterized by how we live our lives before others, how we respond to various circumstances of life. What do we say and how do we react to a flat tire, spilled coffee, or a *C* on a final exam?

"The contribution of Spontaneous Modeling to learning is that we can observe positive expressions of faith in the lives of others. We represent living 'commentaries' of the truth. We answer the question: 'What does God's truth look like in day-to-day living?'...We demonstrate the validity of what it means to be 'Christian' through our intimate relationships with God and others."[39]

Certainly both structured and spontaneous modeling were prominent in youth groups where teens reaching teens for Christ took place on a regular basis. As noted previously students who reached more of their friends for Christ saw someone lead another to Christ roughly every week. Regular exposure to adults leading teens to Christ significantly influences a student leader's effectiveness in leading peers to Christ. More distinctly, if that teen watches another teen lead a peer to Christ, the impact on their witnessing efforts is even more dramatic. Of the students who had helped friends come to Christ, 85 percent said they had seen an adult lead someone to Christ—and 85 percent of *that* group had seen a teen lead a teen to Christ. You can quickly see that modeling how to share the gospel is the most powerful training tool available to help students reach their friends for Jesus Christ. If modeling is necessary for student leader effectiveness, youth workers will need to strategize with this reality in mind.

NONVERBAL INFLUENCE

The old phrase "actions speak louder than words" was never more prominent than in conversations with students about witnessing. Modeling for students took on the form of being a good example. It was the first consideration by most of these students as they talked about their ministry to their peers. They weren't just watching how they acted so that they were faithful in their own walks with God—they were purposefully "exampling" for others. When asked about it, one student quickly exclaimed, "Yes it's important! It's the *hugest* thing!"

As we discussed in Chapter 3, research has shown that the majority of students are inarticulate about their faith.[40] It is normal, then, that students pay such careful attention to how best to communicate—through actions. It may very well be the hugest thing.

Being a good example to nonbelievers was important to student leaders as they strove to witness through their actions and display the impact of their beliefs on their behavior. We discovered it was very important to students that they demonstrated consistency—not only in their moral behavior, but also in how they related to others. Within the social framework of a school or peer group, where various norms and values translate into actions, these student leaders understood the need for harmony between what they believed and how they lived. If contradictions existed between the two, then unbelievers wouldn't be interested in hearing their verbal witness for Christ. There would be no authenticity to the message. Even though it may seem obvious to youth workers, this reality was a big deal to students and part of their conscious efforts to reach their friends.

Being an example also played a key role within the structures of the youth ministries' student *leadership* groups. As student leader teams are formed within a youth ministry, the opinions of other students toward the team can help or hinder the group's ability to lead. If the team gives careful attention to how they're perceived, they can experience even greater impact. For example, when asked why he was a student leader, one teen commented, "I saw the senior guys on leadership team, and I wanted to be like them."

As we dialed in a bit on what being an example involves, the role of encouragement kept coming up. Students were not only examples of what being a Christ follower involved, they were also serving others through the act of encouragement. In the sea of sarcasm that is the local school, adolescents know the value and necessity of being buoyed by peer encouragement. You can see the contagious potential of Christ-centered youth ministries as they truly reflect who Christ is to others versus taking a condemning stance separate from real life.

SOME GO IN GROUPS

Many of these students learned to share their faith through team witnessing, something we don't hear much about these days. Doing prayer walks, where groups walk and pray for particular communities and locations, was the most common approach to help students think missionally about reaching a community. Some of the groups did mall evangelism, which allowed their students both to share their faith and to watch other students in their teams tell others the good news. Almost half the students in our study had been out in teams to share their faith at least once a month. Given that half the students had seldom shared or never shared their faith, this ministry practice certainly seemed like valuable training for the other half to learn how to tell others about Jesus.

Not all youth workers are sold on the idea of a nonrelational approach to evangelism. In fact, our evangelistic priority ought to be with those who we know and are part of our regular circle of acquaintances. We want kids to reach their friends. But on the way toward that natural goal, students often *gain* telling skills through other evangelistic approaches that require them to take initiative. Evangelism Explosion[41] and Dare 2

Share[42] are organizations that train students in clearly sharing the gospel with anyone in a variety of natural contexts, like walking down the street or doing business at a store.

Youth ministries used team witnessing groups of two or more to share the gospel. They went to shopping malls, along streets, or door to door to specific teens' homes. Usually the people they talked to were unknown to the team before they met. After initiating a conversation or asking persons to complete a survey, team members asked a question designed to create interest in listening to a (usually) quick presentation of the gospel. The number of times a prayer for salvation has been prayed in such encounters is staggering.

Students reported there were few ongoing relationships after these encounters, and follow-up was often nonexistent. Of course, there were exceptions. Often the individual shared with was an adult who would never be interested in attending youth group and, as a result, the group members weren't able to report how these people were doing spiritually. The claim by youth leaders who employ these methods is that team witnessing might be the best way to help student leaders combine the desired skills with the required boldness to be effective in their telling. While many youth groups live this out only on mission trips one week a year, some evangelistically committed groups push their students to practice this discipline about once a month in their own neighborhoods.

THE ROLE OF SCRIPTURE

A key distinctive of these groups was the centrality of the Bible. They were committed to providing clear, biblical teaching each week. Scripture was more than just part of the upfront teaching. The students were routinely engaged in personal devotions and Scripture memorization. The teens saw Scripture as a guiding force, one of the main methods of discovering what God expected of them. As they studied and learned from the stories of biblical men and women, they discovered truth applicable to their lives as Christians and as leaders.

However, while Scripture is foundational to a student leader's spiritual growth and development, our research found that Bible reading didn't predict evangelistic activity. Even those who had never played a key role in bringing a friend to Christ had personal devotions a few times each week. There was, however, a significant difference among students who memorized Scripture. Students who had led more than four friends to Christ regularly memorized Scripture. The implications are that these students were not only equipped with tools, they also practiced learning Scripture to use with their friends as they shared. It's most likely that their earliest experiences in sharing with others convinced them of their need to use Scripture to tell the gospel story.

RETREATS, CAMPS, AND CONFERENCES

When it comes to the role of these getaway events, there's a mixed response about their role for evangelistically effective groups. One commonly marketed method is to attend a large conference that focuses on evangelism training. There is evidence to suggest that many of these conferences effectively inspire students to share their faith and do so more often.[43] It was noteworthy, however, that almost all of the youth groups we studied didn't note such conferences as integral to their success. Were conferences seen as effective? Sure. Did these youth groups attend them? Yes. Were they perceived as non-negotiable to their evangelism training strategy? No.

What was integral was the role of retreats and camps, which were viewed as among the most important events that these groups did each year. In fact the groups saw these community-building and God-centered events as important for their own evangelistic success. Part of the reasons for this emerged in the Link Institute study cited earlier. I (Dave) and Tom Bergler discovered that retreats and camps are key places where people make commitments to follow Christ: Those wishing to evangelize teenagers should make use of church camps, retreats, or conferences. Such events are especially important for the conversions of teenagers with little or no religious background, and the events should include a challenge to act—that is, a pointed invitation to take steps to become a Christian. The challenge to act is especially important when trying to evangelize males.

Adults wishing to evangelize teenagers should equip Christian teenagers to invite their non-Christian friends to camps, retreats, or conferences. Such invitations are especially important for the conversions of those with less religious backgrounds.[44]

It's worthwhile to pause and consider the role of retreats and camps in your yearly curriculum and evangelistic strategy. This research points out that they often are targeted for student-leader invitations, and when there's a challenge to act, students respond. Some may feel that retreats are old-fashioned and stuck in 1970s programmatic thinking. Maybe they ought to be one of the primary and regular focal points.

SHORT-TERM MISSION TRIPS

After collecting timed responses from small groups having to arrive at consensus, one finding that jumped out was that these evangelistic youth ministries consistently named short-term mission trips as the activity that contributes most to their evangelistic success. Short-term missions provide powerful opportunities to see God at work and to learn how to rely on the Holy Spirit while reaching out to others.

This finding was so significant that it compelled me (Terry) to focus my doctoral research at Purdue University on how short-term missions work for youth ministry groups.[45] Because most of the effect of short-term missions is based on learning through experience in a foreign culture, the difficulty has been for students to transfer the learning back home, where life is quite different—and routine. Adults can strategically step into the experience of these trips to help students process their learning, providing feedback to help students think through the connections to their own lives.

There is no research to support the notion that participating in short-term missions will make a student a more successful evangelist, but these experiences do seem to play a key communal role in evangelistic youth groups. Adult leaders should give careful consideration to what activities students will do on a short-term mission trip. It's not just that students have short-term missions experiences—it's the quality and content of those experiences that matters.

Those who host short-term mission groups from the United States can quickly tell the heart of the groups they host. While watching a particular youth group in action in Iasi, Romania, a missionary commented to me (Terry), "This group has done more in a week and a half with the street kids than I've had groups come over and do in six weeks." When asked to explain the difference, he noted the students' willingness to work, their willingness and ability to verbally share the gospel, their ability to express love and care cross-culturally, their prepared plan for ministry opportunities, and the evident training they had before they came overseas. Preparation in the direction of mission effectiveness and lasting impact made the difference.

Most of the students in our study reported seeing God work through them on mission trips as they verbally shared the gospel. It became a wake-up call for some to commit their lives to serving God and his purposes. A youth pastor once wrote, "I grew up in a pastor's home and sat through billions of mission conferences. I was mission-conferenced out of my ears, yet it wasn't until my senior year in high school that I went to Venezuela and experienced missions. I didn't go to necessarily minister—I just wanted to see firsthand what a foreign mission field was like. But it was there I got a heart for missions; it was there the Lord called me to ministry of some sort."[46]

This last sentence supports some of the key findings from my (Terry's) doctoral research. These are powerful moments of identity development in the lives of students. Rather than seeing them as training missions for greater verbal witnessing at home or more charitable actions toward the poor, youth workers need to understand that they are more about developing an understanding (confidence and clarity) of what God wants them to do. It's this missional confidence exuded throughout the evangelistic groups we researched that propelled them to make a difference.

As that missional confidence grows within the group, students see God work and rely on him more. When a youth ministry focuses on the important things that change lives—praying hard, inviting often, and explaining well—exciting things can happen. As one student said, "God moves a lot in this youth group and that keeps me going." Another quickly added, "Knowing that each of us has a ministry God is calling us to, we know that people are hearing the gospel because of us."

"But the father said to his servants, 'Quick! Bring the best robe and put it on him. Put a ring on his finger and sandals on his feet. Bring the fattened calf and kill it. Let's have a feast and celebrate. For this son of mine was dead and is alive again; he was lost and is found.' So they began to celebrate." (Luke 15:22-24)

And that's good news!

CHAPTER EIGHT
TRACKING THE CHANGE

Grab a medium-sized potato and head to your microwave oven. Set the timer for 4 minutes, 45 seconds. Grab your favorite toppings, and chances are pretty good you'll be able to eat a tasty baked potato shortly.

But we can't deliver cookbook precision when it comes to empowering students for courageous and contagious faith. These pages aren't recipes for success so much as chefs' notes from a couple of guys who've been stirring the pot for a while in this particular kitchen. Before suggesting some ways we can monitor progress, let's recognize a couple of major limitations to such an ambition.

IMPRECISION IS A REALITY OF LIFE

We didn't specify that by "medium-sized potato" we intended for you to select one of the Idaho variety, weighing between 6 and 7 ounces. But chances are you knew enough to get the right size spud nuked and ready to eat. There were other instructions on which we could have elaborated, leading us to great detail and maybe greater confusion.

The state of religious practice in Israel during Jesus' day is an example of how excessive instruction can be misleading. Ten simple commandments were to be obeyed by God's people. But as teachers started messing with how they could know they were on the right track or in error, they felt they needed more specificity:

Q: *How do we keep the Sabbath holy?*
A: Don't work.

Q: *What do we mean by* work?
A: Well, don't walk too far, for starters.

Q: *How far is "too far"?*
A: If you live in Jerusalem, don't walk outside of the city.

Q: *What, exactly, are the city boundaries, so we're all clear?*
A: Ummm...Bethphage, on the Mount of Olives, is the marker on the east.

Plenty of details, right?

In fact with this common knowledge in place, Jesus stopped at Bethphage and sent two disciples ahead to retrieve the donkey needed for his prophecy-fulfilling Palm Sunday entry into Jerusalem. It was like he waited by the "Welcome to Jerusalem" sign to make sure he did the journey right, and the message was unmistakable to his crowd. *This was the Messiah!*

All of this is cool for us to look back upon because it gives us additional insights about how well Jesus knew what everyone else knew were the standards for obeying YHWH. But the larger truth is that our Lord wrangled with the establishment over these very standards. The Ten Commandments had become so Torah-bloated that remembering and practicing hundreds of laws was the way people tried to love the Lord God with all their heart, soul, mind, and strength. Plenty of precision, but this system was not helpful when it came to actually keeping the main thing the main thing.

A Youth for Christ multi-staff team in a large urban area attempted to standardize what they meant by "follow-up for new Christians." They spelled out 12 steps they want from their staff, starting with a personal phone call within the first 48 hours of a student's decision to trust Jesus as Savior and Lord. The behaviors they encourage from their staff are quite admirable, including working through six chapters in a particular booklet and visiting church twice with the young believer before "handing off" the rest of the discipleship agenda to a local fellowship. Our concern is that as these sorts of explicit standards get practiced, the checklist becomes the target and it's easy to forget that the true goal is much simpler and pervasive. Establishing a new believer in Christ is also naturally resistant to precise measurement. YFC wants previously unchurched teens to become lifelong followers of Jesus. If this ultimate goal doesn't take place, there won't be much comfort in being able to point to stacks of completed 12-step checklists.

The nature of research is such that it drives us past common levels of detail as we gather and make sense of data. One of the key criteria to consider when designing research is the concept of *validity*. This concern has us ask whether what we're trying to measure is, in fact, a good representation of what we really care about. Jesus—and prophets who preceded him—sought to correct the misplaced emphasis of God's people who were so focused on the outward appearances of the law that their hearts were neglected. Religious leaders were tracking the wrong indicators. We'd like to humbly suggest that our YFC friends are making a similar error. The 12 steps simply aren't valid predictors that the true desired outcome—raising lifelong disciples of Christ—will be achieved.

It can be tempting to seek precise indicators of progress for our biggest pursuits. There's great risk we will agree on standards simply because they are clear and there will be no confusion. Though we obviously care about how we'll track progress, we don't want to sell out for measurement shortcuts that help us feel good about what we do in the short term though we have no idea if we're on target for the long haul.

Our truest desire is captured by the oft-repeated and un-packed phrase of this book. We want to *empower students for a courageous and contagious faith*. When we do so, students will grow into leadership-as-influence with their friends. And their friends who don't yet know Christ will be drawn into a relationship with him. Leadership and evangelism effective-ness will be observable outcomes. Our research has shown that individual student patterns of praying, inviting, and tell-ing are related to these outcomes. A combination of these indicators and others to be discussed in this chapter will give us a constellation for tracking changes that has validity and represents our most important focus.

THERE ARE ALWAYS VARIABLES

How powerful is your microwave? That will affect the amount of time it takes to cook your potato just right. And there truly are a lot of differences between potatoes, so that will be a fac-tor in your setting. Of course, in the end you will likely make adjustments based on the most important variable of all: Your taste preferences.

A second important consideration for research design and implementation is *reliability*. We know there are always variables. But by adding some controls to these differences, we can increase our confidence that the information we've gathered is an accurate representation of what we want to measure.

Imagine the number of different variables that come into play when we try to measure ministry-related impact in the young people with whom we work. Is a particular teen beginning to share his faith with his friend because of the training we did last weekend? (That is, after all, why we do such things!) Our research has identified a number of other possible reasons for his new behavior. It may simply be that someone close to him—a parent, youth pastor, or another friend—has been modeling evangelistic activity, and this influence is beginning to take hold. The frequency of this young man's personal growth behaviors, including Bible study and prayer, may have increased over the last few months, putting his heart in a position to act more courageously with his friends. Maybe the quality of supportive programming has improved so that he's experienced success inviting lost friends into a place where spiritual conversations are a smaller step instead of a giant leap. The factors that have empowered this guy to live out a more contagious faith may be due to changes in his character, behavior, attitudes, circumstances, environment, friends' receptivity, friends' life situations, the encouragement he experiences, better programming—the list goes on. If we want to accurately assess something, we have to recognize the challenge of isolating what we want to measure.

That's why we so often default to easily counted numbers, such as looking to attendance as an indicator of effectiveness. Attendance patterns might not represent exactly what we care about (validity), but at least we can have confidence in their accuracy (reliability).

Our research design may be an instructive help toward understanding the kind of care needed to isolate variables and ensure accuracy when we try to assess how well we're doing in ministry. We planned for multiple ways of collecting information about students who were effective at reaching their friends for Christ, always trying to cluster these indicators around the target of measurement we really cared about. And we spelled out clearly what this target was, an exercise that should never be taken too lightly as we approach the task of ministry assessment. Two questions captured our focus: 1) *What are the differences between student leaders who reach their friends for Christ and those who don't? and 2) What are the common factors in youth ministries where teens reaching teens for Christ is the norm?*

At the outset we used extensive ministry networks to solicit nominations for student ministries with a reputation for raising up and empowering young people for peer influence. We added some qualifiers to this referral-seeking process in order to get a close-up view of ministries that had consistently demonstrated the development of teens for evangelistic effectiveness. So we established some criteria to limit the number of variables that would come into play: To be eligible for study, a ministry needed to be at least three years old and have retained the same adult leadership for those three years. When the dust settled on this phase of our research, we had collected 109 referrals.

We then conducted phone interviews with the groups' leaders who possessed a reputation for student-leader excellence, assigning each to one of three categories: 1) Perfect fit, must visit, 2) Good fit, visit if we can afford to, 3) Not a good fit for our research focus. These categories allowed us to identify which ministries were most representative of the type of group we wanted to investigate. This winnowing process was an exercise toward increasing reliability. In a sense we were more specifically identifying what we meant by a medium-size potato. We used our two focus questions as the filter for these determinations.

During spring 1997 we joined with 10 Huntington University students and divided into teams to visit the 17 ministries that best met our criteria. Time and money constraints were also considerations when planning the visits.

At least two people—and often more—visited each site. Simply having multiple eyes and ears in the process helped to ensure greater accuracy in data collection. (We'll later describe how the ability to compare notes with team members led to a rewarding and unpredicted potential finding.)

While on location we collected information through individual surveys, small focus groups, and large-group discussions. Multiple strategies helped ensure the reliability of data, allowing more qualitative forms (discussions, interviews, open-ended questions) to help us understand the answers to multiple-choice survey questions regarding the frequency of students' key behaviors.

After some analysis of this data, we formulated hypotheses to explain what we'd found. But we felt the need to test these tentative conclusions, and we were also interested in adding ministry sites that were more representative of the diversity around the country. Again, both of these moves were intended to give us a more accurate body of information to help us understand what we were most interested in learning.

During the winter of 1997-1998 we revisited two of the previous year's locations and traveled to an additional five sites. We performed additional individual interviews and tweaked our discussions to further explore our hypotheses. All in all, 424 high school students from 22 different youth ministries scattered across the country participated in our study. These young people came from student leadership teams ranging in size from six to 51, and represented youth ministries with official rolls from 80 to 850. Attendance at the largest weekly events for these groups ranged from 35 to 350.

The visits gave us a fertile combination of statistical data, small-group reports, observations, adult staff and youth pastor interviews, and detailed one-on-one interviews. Most important to the point of this discussion: We have confidence that our information is reliable enough to form the backbone of this book and guide contemporary student ministry practices, especially as it relates to our central desire of empowering students for a courageous and contagious faith.[47]

STAGES OF VITALITY: A SURPRISE FINDING WORTH CONSIDERATION

A true story from our research journey together illustrates how we can combine our artistic and intuitive perceptions with research disciplines to arrive at reliable conclusions about the progress we may or may not be making. Many youth ministers have found these findings to be a useful feedback tool for them as they endeavor to locate indicators of progress for their group's spiritual vitality.

We had just visited a youth ministry for a second time, a year after part of the team had collected data there and left very impressed. Both of us went on this second trip, taking all four of the sharp Huntington students we had invited to work with us during this additional year of research. While on location this time, we conducted large-group and individual interviews, an effort to add some qualitative data[48] to the mix.

As we sat in the airport waiting to head home, we were troubled that our interviews hadn't generated the language associated with a passion for reaching others as we had expected. The impressiveness from the first visit wasn't as evident the second time. We began to theorize that groups may actually reveal something of their spiritual vitality through the qualitative data—what they choose to talk about and why. Some groups may be good at building unity. Others may be good at keeping kids "safe," while others shared an expectancy that God would use them to reach out to their schools and neighborhoods.

After much discussion and a review of the data, the research team agreed on four various stages along a continuum that represented what we were hearing. A group could progress from one to the next, reflecting a greater level of spiritual vitality in each one. We had every team member assign each youth group to one of these stages of vitality, averaged those rankings, and then assigned each youth ministry into the stage determined by this collective process.

By running a statistical analysis of the quantitative survey, we were able to see if there were any marked differences between the groups. This was essentially a second test of what we had picked up by listening carefully. The first checkpoint was to learn that all of our team members detected these same distinctive stages, or patterns, in the answers that groups provided. Now we were testing the possibility that our collective perceptions could be verified by the other scientific means we had at our disposal. We were curious to see if there was a connection between the identified spiritual vitality and fruitfulness of groups and the language they used in their conversations and discussions.

Before sharing what we found, we want to reiterate that our intent is not to be critical of any of the youth ministries participating in our research. Like any good crime scene investigator, we are simply reporting the facts. It was a privilege to be granted access to some of the best youth ministries in the country, and we owe it to them to be faithful in revealing what we uncovered and hopeful that there is wide benefit from being aware of how groups may exhibit a collective profile of spiritual vitality. A goal for any group should be to move from self-centered tendencies toward greater maturity and faithfulness—resulting in more fruitful outreach. The language used by groups can be an indicator of their spiritual vitality.

We found statistically significant evidence for clearly defining the first three stages of vitality. The fourth stage, while supported clearly by the qualitative data, was not differentiated by statistical measures (most likely due to the statistical power limitations of a relatively small sample size being considered in this fourth stage). What we did find was a big gulf between the Peer Encouragement stage and the God-at-Work stage—a significant difference that focused on the prayer practices and approach to personal insecurities regarding their evangelistic practices.

STAGES OF VITALITY

1. LOVE FLOWING STAGE

A loving and caring atmosphere is established so that most group members and visitors affirm its presence.

2. PEER ENCOURAGEMENT STAGE

Peer ministry is so normal that students easily cite one-anothering examples of helping each other grow in their faith.

THE BIG GULF

A significant difference in language and expectancy that God will work.

4. EVANGELISM EXPECTANCY STAGE

The expectation that God will be at work includes a strong anticipation that God will use them to reach others.

3. GOD-AT-WORK STAGE

Students report as normal that God intervenes in their lives to powerfully answer prayer.

We gave each stage a name that described the dominant emphasis for the group members and leaders. The Love Flowing stage is what we found as a basic foundation of the healthy student ministries in our research, where a loving and caring atmosphere is established so that most members and visitors affirm its presence. The borders of the youth group were clearly defined such that each member knew who was in and who was not. Members prayed when they gathered each week, but they typically didn't invite visitors and seldom prayed for opportunities to share with others.

The second stage, Peer Encouragement, was the description we attached to most of the groups participating in our research. The predominant feature of this stage is that peer ministry exists to the point where students could easily cite "one anothering" examples of how students in the group helped others grow in their faith. Groups fitting this description not only worked at unity, but also shared notable experiences together and cared for one another in substantial ways. They were purposeful communities with healthy images among their peers at school. The students worked hard to keep the youth ministries warm, active, and fresh. But notably, they didn't evidence much praying activity for opportunities to share their faith with others. They basically possessed an internal focus on the health of their own groups.

Don't miss the fact that most of these students were thinking about encouraging those who already belonged to their group—not how to reach out to others. Although healthy ministries clearly can take place at this stage, we think there is something very important being neglected. And the growth that's missing is catalyzed primarily by a change in the prayer patterns within the group.

How do groups move from this stage of taking care of their own to the place where they expand their influence? We've come to understand that the big gulf to navigate is for student groups to overcome their personal fears and share their faith with their friends. When they do so, chances are they've moved into the God-at-Work stage, characterized by the intentional prayers of students and adults together for such breakthroughs. This activity has the result of moving the focus off of themselves and their own membership and onto what God may want to do through them as they depend on him by faith.

In this God-at-Work stage there was an atmosphere of expectancy regarding the work of God so that students report as normal that God intervenes in their lives to powerfully answer prayer. Groups characterized by this stage easily expressed their trust in God during their conversations. They communicated that the Lord was still interested in drawing people to himself. In fact, they couldn't keep from calling attention to the evidence of their love for God and—more importantly— how God had been working to change their friends' lives. One teen from such a student ministry shared, "You cannot walk into our youth group without noticing God."

Behaviorally, they set themselves apart from other groups by aggressively initiating prayer and improving their witness to their communities. As a result they experienced a tighter community of faith than did others. Students who were part of these groups were self-motivated to pray, not waiting for adults to organize their efforts. There was a clear difference in prayer at this stage; it was not so much a collection of individualized approaches as it was a true standard of community behavior. One young person told us, "Prayer [in this group] is big, both individually and corporately. Some meet every day for prayer during lunch at school. This is a close-knit community." These God-at-Work student ministries not only prayed more intentionally to be a witness, they followed up by providing intentional training and activities that would help their students share their faith with their friends.

There were a few groups that we found in the final stage of Evangelism Expectancy. Students in these ministries prayed almost daily for opportunities to share their faith. They were a more seasoned version of the groups in the God-at-Work stage. One of the distinctive characteristics of this group was that they memorized Scripture more than teens from other groups. God's Word circulates throughout their lives in ways that inform their prayers, reminding us of the words of the Psalmist, "[Blessed are those] who delight in the law of the LORD and meditate on his law day and night" (Psalm 1:2).

Listening to how students speak to one another will supply rich insights about what's going on in a group. Chances are pretty good that this sort of attentiveness will be useful in making judgments about the kind of values around which the group is being socialized (see Chapter 4). As we seek to empower students for a courageous and contagious faith, it seems clear that we'd love to hear conversations that fall into the God-at-Work stage. Such language testifies to the reality that significant values of prayer, love for the lost, and God's Word have taken root in our students.

HOPE FOR THE FUTURE

Research findings have been introduced and discussed in this book, all of it in support of a specific and compelling youth ministry vision. We want to see teens empowered by the courageous hearts we help nurture in them so they can live their faith openly and contagiously among their friends. If groups live into these values, they'll begin to exhibit characteristics like those just discussed in the God-at-Work stage, and their friends will join them as followers of Jesus Christ.

Other indicators of such spiritual vitality have been talked about. Adults will model courageous hearts by making their own faith-driven decisions of integrity and sharing them with appropriate transparency. They will show young people how to overcome their fears and display contagious lives of influence on behalf of the Lord Jesus. Consistent and dependable outreach programs will be provided by such adults, but they will most significantly be involved in the lives of students as mentors, coaching them from Scripture on how to live for the Lord. Paying attention to how well the adult teams working with young people are shaping up is a great place to start as we look for signs of progress.

Simple but powerful patterns of praying, inviting, and explaining provide reliable clues to each individual student's effectiveness in reaching their friends for Christ and helping them grow in Christ. These patterns are so substantive that we concentrated much of this book toward unpacking their value and describing their behavioral indicators. And we also learned that students who exert evangelistic influence on their friends are also less likely to be invested in program planning and leadership; it distracts them from the more substantive role of loving their friends well enough to reveal the hope of Christ in up-close and personal ways.

Finally, we've seen a picture of what groups might look like if they adopt a way of doing student ministry that takes seriously the evangelistic mission of God. From the values of prayer, love, God's Word, and unity to specific stages of vitality as described in this chapter, we can begin to describe the outcome we're after. The vision is becoming clear.

In the end, that's our prayer for this book. We hope the details and discussion of these pages will launch a different, deeper way of doing youth ministry. We want to advocate for empowering young people from the inside out, concentrating on forming their hearts to be courageous for Christ and then leading them to live into the mission of God, contagious in their faith, making a difference in their world.

Many are troubled by the current state of churches in America, wondering if we haven't slipped off center. If there is reason for such concern, we have confidence that empowering students today for a courageous and contagious faith is our best—and most faithful—move for a church tomorrow that makes Jesus proud.

May we be found faithful, Father.

APPENDIX: RESEARCH TOOLS

THE PHONE TEMPLATE

Interviewer_____

Church _____

City _____

Youth Pastor _____

Phone _____

Years YP has been at church _____

Average attendance at youth activities:

Middle School _____High School _____

"Hi, I'm _____ from Huntington College's Link Institute for faithful and effective youth ministry. I'm part of a research team that's taking a look at factors that contribute to the effectiveness of high school Christians as they try to influence their classmates for Jesus Christ. Some groups call this "student leadership," but we don't want to get hung up on labels just now. Your group was nominated to us as a result of the first stage of our research, where we sought input from a wide range of national youth ministry networks.

The purpose of this call is to see if there is a time in this next week that I might be able to schedule a call back for a 20-minute interview that will assist us in the next stage of our research."

- -

"We're interested in learning something about the normal patterns of activity your teens who are leaders are involved in.

a) First, how many students do you have involved in student leadership of some form or another?

b) What is your definition of student leadership?

c) If your sharpest students were asked to describe what it means for them to be student leaders, what would they say?

d) For how many of these students do you have knowledge that they are actively working (prayer, building relationships, small groups with nonbelievers, accountability witnessing partnerships, sharing their faith, planning and leading outreach programs, etc.) toward reaching their peers for Christ?

e) Think of the school year thus far. Of those kids who may have come to Christ thus far, how many might you attribute to the active work of one or more of your student leaders? (Can they describe some details?)

f) Even now, could you identify any fresh activity that some of your students may be currently involved in to reach their peers for Christ? (Can they describe some details?)

g) How would you describe your ongoing role (and that of other adult leaders) in the lives of your student leaders?

h) For how many of your student leaders are you convinced that, right now, if adult influence and support were withdrawn, they would continue to take initiative to reach their peers for Christ?

i) For how many years would you say that you have had student leaders who are regularly involved in reaching their peers for Christ?

j) How many of the leaders in your group that you know who reach out to non-Christians became Christians themselves under your ministry?

k) (*To the interviewer: If you like what you're hearing, ask this question. If not, skip it.*) What things did you do in your ministry to get to this point where peers reaching peers for Christ is happening regularly? (Get thorough answers here.)

l) Can you briefly describe your monthly ministry schedule?

m) Would you describe your setting—schools involved, church is located, etc.?

n) Would you be willing to have a team of two to four people from Huntington College come visit and do more research with you and your students?

(We'd like to get some stories here. If it seems like some peer-to-peer stuff is happening, have them tell you a couple of the better ones where a teen reached a teen for Christ and write them as thoroughly as possible.)

Make sure to end the conversation by thanking them for their time.

Now, after you've hung up: What were your impressions of the call?

The youth ministry there?

The youth pastor/contact?

In your estimation, is this or isn't this a place where we ought to go see what's going on?

HUNTINGTON COLLEGE LINK INSTITUTE STUDENT LEADER RESEARCH PROJECT

FORCED CHOICE RESPONSE INTERVIEW

Please take a few minutes to answer the following questions by checking the box that most accurately represents what you believe.

For how many of your friends who have come to Christ would you say you played a key role?

☐ none   ☐ 1-3   ☐ 4-8   ☐ more than 8

How did you come to put your faith in Christ?

☐ parents/family

☐ one-on-one with youth pastor/staff

☐ one-on-one with an adult

☐ one-on-one with another teen

☐ I was by myself

☐ through a youth group program/event

☐ other

What is the most important thing you do as a leader in your youth group?

☐ invite friends

☐ encourage others

☐ provide up-front leadership

☐ lead a small group

☐ meet with other leaders

☐ plan meetings/activities

☐ share my faith

What has been the biggest personal obstacle you've faced to your leading others to Christ?

☐ my own fears   ☐ my lack of training

☐ my busy schedule   ☐ I need someone to get me started

What has helped you the most to become a person who works at leading others to Christ?

☐ youth pastor/key adult   ☐ my parent(s)

☐ Christian friends   ☐ youth group meetings

☐ special conference   ☐ missions trip

☐ my own experiences   ☐ small group meetings

What is most helpful to you as you try to convince your friends to put their faith in Christ?

☐ adults who care   ☐ leadership team

☐ other friends   ☐ youth group meetings

☐ special conferences   ☐ special trips/retreats

☐ special activities   ☐ small group meetings

For each of the following statements, please place a check in the **ONE** box that most accurately reflects what your personal experiences have been *in the last six months.*

I pray for opportunities to tell someone about Jesus.

I pray specifically for one particular friend to become a Christian.

I pray with others so that our specific friends will become Christians.

I organize others to pray for specific friends who need to become Christians.

I do some things just so I can build friendships with classmates who aren't Christians.

I invite non-Christian friends to large group activities where I know they will learn about Jesus.

I invite non-Christian friends to join me in a small group where they will learn about Jesus.

I invite non-Christian friends to talk with me about Jesus.

I invite non-Christian friends to talk about Jesus with an adult friend I know.

I help plan events where non-Christians can hear about Jesus.

I tell my non-Christian friends what my personal relationship with Jesus Christ means to me.

I pray with non-Christian friends for special problems.

NEVER HAPPENS	SELDOM HAPPENS	ABOUT MONTHLY	ABOUT WEEKLY	FEW TIMES WEEKLY	ABOUT DAILY	FEW TIMES DAILY

I explain to non-Christians how they can begin a relationship with Jesus Christ.

I pray with non-Christians when they ask Jesus to come into their life.

I hang out with my church friends.

I am involved in church-related activities.

I read the Bible on my own.

I memorize Scripture.

I've seen a teenage friend lead an individual into a personal relationship with Jesus Christ.

I've seen an adult lead an individual into a personal relationship with Jesus Christ.

I've seen one of my parents lead an individual into a personal relationship with Jesus Christ.

I've been coached or trained by an adult about how to share my faith with others.

I've been coached or trained by another teen about how to share my faith with others.

I've met with an adult individually to talk about my own walk with the Lord.

I've gone out with a team of friends for the single purpose of sharing our faith.

NEVER HAPPENS	SELDOM HAPPENS	ABOUT MONTHLY	ABOUT WEEKLY	FEW TIMES WEEKLY	ABOUT DAILY	FEW TIMES DAILY

TIMED TEAM RESPONSES

SMALL GROUP

You will have exactly five minutes to complete each of the questions below. Please wait till the leader tells you to begin on each one and, upon completion of each assignment below, wait until they tell you to begin the next assignment. Please attempt to come up with your group's best responses for each of these questions before writing them down.

A. *Assume that many people who watch this youth ministry agree: This youth ministry is extremely effective on behalf of the kingdom of God. In the next five minutes, this group is to agree upon and write down NO MORE THAN the three most important factors contributing to that ministry effectiveness. You may write less than three, but please do not write more than three factors.*

1.

2.

3.

B. *In the next five minutes, this group is to identify and agree upon the three most important historical events that have taken place in the life of this ministry during the last two years. Write down NO MORE THAN three; you may write less than three, but please do not write down more than three events.*

1.

2.

3.

C. *Imagine that this group has a chance to offer practical advice to other youth ministries all around the country about HOW to help young people reach their classmates for Jesus Christ. In the next five minutes, this group needs to agree upon and write down NO MORE THAN three sentences representing this advice. You may write less than three, but please do not write down more than three statements of advice.*

1.

2.

3.

D. *In the next five minutes, this group is to identify and agree upon the three most important truths or themes that have been taught or discussed in your group during the past year. Write down NO MORE THAN three; you may write less than three, but please do not write down more than three of these truths or themes.*

    1.

    2.

    3.

LINK INSTITUTE
NATIONAL STUDENT LEADERSHIP
RESEARCH PROJECT

ROUND TWO INTERVIEW TEMPLATE

I. DEMOGRAPHICS

Gender? male_____ female_____ *Grade?*_____

For how many of your friends who have come to Christ would you say you played a key role?

none_____ 1-3_____ 4-8_____ more than 8_____

What groups are you involved in at your school?

student council_____ class officer_____ sports_____

band_____ drama_____ academic_____

not much_____ other (specify)_____

If you have a part-time job, about how many hours per week do you work?

don't have job_____ 1-9_____ 10-15_____

16-20_____ more than 20 _____

What position or offices have you held at your school?

president _____ captain of sports team_____

vice president_____ secretary_____

club officer_____ other (specify)_____

none_____

How would you describe your role on the youth group's ministry team?

vocal leader_____   helper/behind the scenes_____

worker _____   creative person _____

loner _____   prayer warrior _____

other _____   youth pastor's helper _____

II. INTERVIEW QUESTIONS

1) *Looking back over your last 6 months of involvement with (_____), how many friends have you invited to a (_____) meeting who were not already involved?*

    1a) **...1 or more**
    Why? Why did you invite others to (_____)?

    ...zero
    Why? What has kept you from bringing friends to (_____)?

    1b) *What about your group gave you confidence that it would be okay socially to invite your friends? (Be sure to probe beyond "unity.")*

    1c) *What about your group gave you confidence that it would help your friends find Christ if you invited them?*

    1d) *How would kids at school describe your youth group?*

2) Do you consider it important that student leaders are good examples in their Christian life? (Probe.)

3) Do you have any regular one-on-one meeting time with an adult where you are helped to grow in your faith and responsibility as a student leader?

> 3a) Who? (no name necessary) What role does this person play in your life? Ex: father, pastor, etc.

> 3b) How did this meeting first come about? When? What goes on? Describe details.

> 3c) Are you held accountable in any way? Describe.

4) Have you ever seen someone lead a person to Christ?

> 4a) **...yes**
> Any chance it was the person you meet with one-on-one?
>
> **...no**
> How do you think that could help you as a student leader?

> 4b) Any chance it was a teenage peer?

> 4c) Describe what you remember.

5) Have you ever individually led another student to faith in Jesus Christ?

> 5a) **...yes**
> How? What one thing do you think was most instrumental in the process of leading them to Christ?

...no

Why not? What one thing would you say was missing that you think would have "opened the door" to lead a peer to Christ?

6) *What is the one personal experience or training event that most effectively developed you to be a student leader who reaches your friends for Christ? Describe.*

    6a)   *What one experience or training strategy from this point forward do you believe would most contribute to your growth as a student leader who reaches others for Christ?*

7) *Describe what role (if any) missions or service trips have played in your development as a student leader.*

8) *What is the philosophy of (<u>youth ministry's name</u>)? How would you describe its purposes?*

9) *As a student leader, are you clear about what is expected of you? Please explain.*

    9a)   *Are the expectations just described the same for everyone who is a student leader, or are there some differences?*

    9b)   *How are these expectations communicated to you?*

    9c)   *Do you have contracts or covenants?*

END NOTES

1. Christian Smith, Denton Smith, and Melinda Lundquist, *Soul Searching: The Religious and Spiritual Lives of American Teenagers* (New York: Oxford, 2005).

2. T. E. Bergler and D. R. Rahn, Results of a collaborative research project in gathering evangelism stories. *Journal of Youth Ministry* 4 (2) (2006), 64-72.

3. C. A. Kress, "Youth Leadership and Youth Development: Connections and Questions," New Directions for Youth Development 109 (2006), 45-56.

4. K. L. Smith, *Ohio 4-H teen leadership. http://ohioline.osu.edu/4-H/tl7.html* (Accessed August 12, 2008).

5. Kress, 46.

6. Laurence Steinberg, *Adolescence*, 6th ed. (Boston: McGraw-Hill, 2002), 300-301.

7. For more on the wide variety of definitions of leadership, see M. Klau, "Exploring Youth Leadership in Theory and Practice," New Directions for Youth Development, 109 (2006), 57-87.

8. David Elkind, *All Grown Up & No Place to Go* (Addison-Wesley, 1984), 33.

9. Rolf Muuss, *Theories of Adolescence*, 5th ed. (Boston: McGraw-Hill, 1988), 273-274.

10. While it clearly isn't as acute, Elkind's idea of the "imaginary audience" isn't just for adolescents. Research has shown that adults struggle with this, too! See J. M. Buis and D. N. Thompson, "A Test of Two Theories: Elkind and Lapsley on the Imaginary Audience and Personal Fable" (paper presented at the annual meeting of the American Educational Research Association, New Orleans, La., April 5-9, 1988). See also M. Quadrel, B. Fischoff, and W. Davis, "Adolescent (in)vulnerability," *American Psychologist* 48 (1993), 102-116, and L. Steinberg, *Adolescence*, 7th ed. (Boston: McGraw-Hill, 2002), 63.

11. Jeffrey Jensen Arnett was the first to point to this reality. For more, see J. J. Arnett, "Emerging Adulthood: A Theory of Development from the Late Teens Through the Twenties," *American Psychologist* 55 (2000), 469-480. Also J. J. Arnett, *Adolescence and Emerging Adulthood: A Cultural Approach* (Upper Saddle River, N.J.: Prentice Hall, 2001). Also J. J. Arnett, Readings on *Adolescence and Emerging Adulthood* (Upper Saddle River, N.J.: Prentice Hall, 2002).

12. Muuss, Chapter 3 on Erickson's theory of identity development.

13. Jesus' first period of ministry lasts approximately eight months, and during the second period of ministry—a 15-month period—he chose the twelve apostles. Bruce M. Metzger, *The New Testament, Its Background, Growth, and Content* (Nashville: Abingdon Press, 1965) 113-115.

14. Muuss.

15. Dave Rahn, "Moral Development in the '80s: Implications for Research and Teaching in Christian Education" (unpublished, 1990).

16. Dave Rahn, "Faith Domain Distinctions in the Conceptualization of Morality and Social Convention for Evangelical Christians" (unpublished doctoral dissertation, 1991).

17. "Trends in the Prevalence of Sexual Behaviors: National YRBS 1991-2007," Centers for Disease Control. *www.cdc.gov/HealthyYouth/yrbs/pdf/yrbs07_us_sexual_behaviors_trend.pdf*

18. "Brook's position on young people's sexual activity," Brook Advisory Centres. *www.brook.org.uk/content/M6_4_sexualactivity.asp*

19. "Facts and Statistics: Sexual Health and Canadian Youth," Society of Obstetricians and Gynaecologists of Canada. *www.sexualityandu.ca/teachers/data-1.aspx*

20. "U.S. Teen Sexual Activity," Kaiser Family Foundation, January 2005. www.kff.org/youthhivstds/upload/U-S-Teen-Sexual-Activity-Fact-Sheet.pdf

21. "Sexual Health Statistics for Teenagers and Young Adults in the United States," Kaiser Family Foundation, September 2006. *www.kff.org/womenshealth/upload/3040-03.pdf*

22. We are grateful to Dr. Ted Bryant, assistant professor of psychology (and amazing youth ministry volunteer) at Bethel College (Ind.) for his input.

23. A helpful book in educational psychology is *How We Learn: A Christian Teacher's Guide to Educational Psychology* by Klaus Issler and Ronald Habermas (WIPF & Stock Publishers, 2002). A more practical book for youth ministry that is built on solid educational psychology approaches is *Teaching the Bible Creatively: How to Awaken Your Kids to Scripture* by Bill McNabb and Steve Mabry (Zondervan, 1990).

24. For more on brain research, start with Frontline episode "Inside the Teenage Brain" (PBS, 2000). *www.pbs.org/wgbh/pages/frontline/shows/teenbrain/work/adolescent.html.* Check out this overview by Nora Underwood, "The Teenage Brain," *The Walrus, www.walrusmagazine.com/articles/2006.11-science-the-teenage-brain/1/* (Thanks, Marko). Or see this fact sheet: "Adolescent Brain Development," Research Facts and Findings, Cornell University, May 2002,

www.actforyouth.net/documents/may02factsheetadolbraindev.pdf.
If you want more read *Primal Teen: What the New Discoveries about the Teenage Brain Tell Us about Our Kids* by Barbara Strauch (Bantam Double-day Dell, 2004).

25. See Issler and Habermas, *How We Learn: A Christian Teacher's Guide to Educational Psychology* for more on spontaneous and structured modeling.

26. This Socialization Values section has borrowed and adapted from Dave Rahn's earlier chapter in Ronald Habermas' *Introduction to Christian Education and Formation: A Lifelong Plan for Christ-Centered Restoration* (Grand Rapids, Mich.: Zondervan, 2008).

27. Charles R. Swindoll, *The Grace Awakening* (Waco, Texas: Word, 1990), 220-221.

28. Jim Cymbala, *Fresh Wind, Fresh Fire* (Grand Rapids, Mich.: Zondervan, 1997), 71.

29. Alan Hirsch, *The Forgotten Ways: Reactivating the Missional Church* (Grand Rapids, Mich.: Brazos Press, 2006), 34.

30. This was a common strategy in Jim Henderson's *Evangelism Without Additives: What if Sharing Your Faith Meant Just Being Yourself?* (Colorado Springs, Colo.: WaterBrook Press, 2007).

31. Rosalind Rinker, *Prayer: Conversing with God* (Grand Rapids, Mich.: Zondervan, 1973), 45.

32. Dave Rahn and Youth for Christ, *3Story: Preparing for a Lifestyle of Evangelism* (Grand Rapids, Mich.: Zondervan/Youth Specialties, 2007).

33. B. J. Kallenberg, *Live to Tell: Evangelism in a Postmodern World* (Grand Rapids, Mich.: Brazos Press, 2002), 54.

34. Hirsch, 94.

35. Kallenberg, 38.

36. See the following:

• "Appendix One: Canadian Non-Christian Affiliation," Transforming Our Nation, *www.outreach.ca/OC6-Resources/download/TON/17%20Appendix %201.pdf*

• "Domestic Missionaries Are Greatly Needed!" The Navigators, *www.navigators.org/us/staff/scalabrin/items/Domestic%20Missionaries%20 Greatly%20Needed!*

• "Church Planting: Get Out There!" Church Planting Village, *www.churchplantingvillage.net/site/c.iiJTKZPEJpH/b.848885/k.A7A6/ Get_Out_There.htm*

37. Mark Dever, *The Gospel and Personal Evangelism* (Wheaton, Ill.: Crossway Books, 2007), 14.

38. Robert Coleman, *The Master Plan of Evangelism* (Old Tappan, N.J.: Fleming H. Revell Company, 1963), 17.

39. Klaus Issler and Robert Habermas, *How We Learn* (Grand Rapids, Mich.: Baker Books, 1994), 83-85.

40. Smith, Smith, and Lundquist, 131. Also T. E. Bergler and D. R. Rahn, Results of a collaborative research project in gathering evangelism stories, *Journal of Youth Ministry* 4(2) (2006), 64-72.

41. www.youthee.org

42. www.dare2share.org

43. Dave Rahn, DC/LA '97 Research Project, unpublished (Huntington, Ind.: Link Institute, August 1998).

44. T. E. Bergler and D. R. Rahn, Results of a collaborative research project in gathering evangelism stories, *Journal of Youth Ministry* 4(2) (2006), 72.

45. For more on Terry's work on short-term missions, check out these publications:

• T. Linhart, "They Were So Alive!: The Spectacle Self and Youth Group Short-term Mission Trips," *Missiology*, 4 (2006): 451-462.

• T. Linhart, "Planting Seeds: The Curricular Hope for Short-term Mission Experience in Youth Ministry," *Christian Education Journal*, Series 3, 2(2) (2005): 256-272.

• T. Linhart, "Do Short-term Mission Trips Make a Long-term Impact?" *Group* (May/June 2005): 93-97.

46. P. Hansen, "Are Youth Mission Trips Biblical?" *Youthworker* 6(2), (1989), 48.

47. More detail about the methods used in our original research, which was the basis of Terry's master's culmination project, can be found in our first book dedicated to the publication of these findings, *Contagious Faith: Empowering Student Leadership in Youth Evangelism* (Loveland, Colo., Group Publishing, 2000).

48. Qualitative research focuses on the text and gives meaning to "findings." It is more than just survey words, but researchers can do solid theoretical work from qualitative data. Terry did this in his doctoral work on short-term missions. For an example, read "Grounded Theory as Scientific Methodology in Youth Ministry Research," *The Journal of Youth Ministry* 1(2), (2003), 27-33.

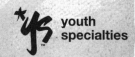

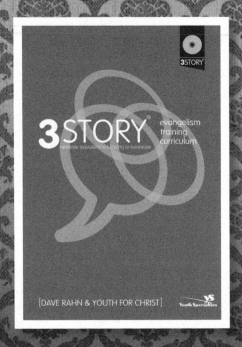

This curriculum course (based on Youth For Christ's 3Story training) offers an interactive learning experience that equips students to live and practice the 3Story way of life—a biblically based, culturally relevant form of discipleship-evangelism. With eight 50-minute training sessions, this curriculum kit is an ideal resource for teaching students how to build deep, authentic relationships with Jesus and genuine, transparent relationships with their friends

3Story® Evangelism Training Curriculum
Preparing Teenagers for a Lifestyle of Evangelism

Youth For Christ
Retail $99.99
978-0-310-27370-7

Visit www.youthspecialties.com
or your local bookstore

youth
specialties

In this DVD series from the Skit Guys, you'll find six weeks of everything you need to teach a memorable lesson to your students on topics that really matter to them. Tommy & Eddie provide you with a Skit Guys video, a message outline, and small group questions for six different lessons on each DVD—making it easier than ever for you to plan a lesson!

You Teach Volume 1
978-0-310-28084-2

You Teach Volume 2
978-0-310-28085-9

You Teach Volume 3
978-0-310-28086-6

You Teach Volume 4
978-0-310-28087-3

The Skit Guys
Retail $19.99 each

Visit www.youthspecialties.com
or your local bookstore.

youth
specialties

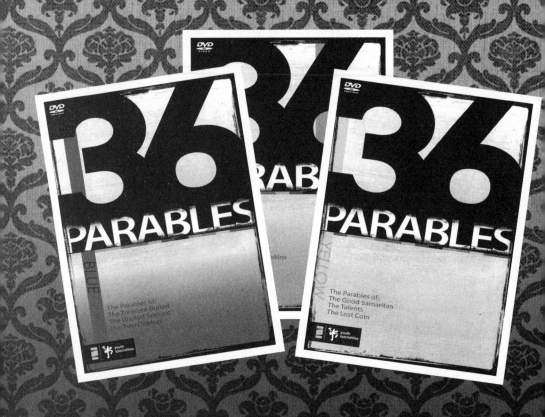

Jesus used parables to teach truth through everyday situations. Now you can retell His timeless stories with a modern twist. 36 Parables uses compelling short films to connect with students and lead them to the truths found in the parables. Use these thought-provoking films as introductions, illustrations, or discussion starters, and your students will see God's Word in a whole new way.

36 Parables
Blue
978-0-310-28083-5

36 Parables
Yellow
978-0-310-28078-1

36 Parables
Cyan
978-0-310-28077-4

Retail $19.99 each

Visit www.youthspecialties.com
or your local bookstore.

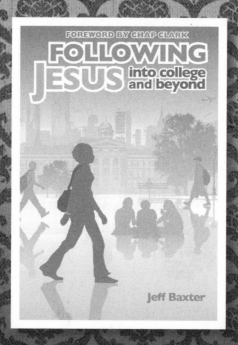

Without a solid faith foundation in a constantly changing society, students risk being pulled in a direction they shouldn't go. Helping students discover who they are and where they're headed, *Following Jesus into College and Beyond* tackles the questions students need to answer to prepare for the rest of their lives as spiritually mature adults.

Following Jesus into College and Beyond

Jeff Baxter
Retail $16.99
978-0-310-28263-1

In *Youth Ministry 3.0*, you'll explore, along with Mark Oestreicher and the voices of other youth workers, why we need change in youth ministry. You'll get a quick history of youth ministry over the last fifty years. And you'll help dream about what changes need to take place in order to create the next phase of youth ministry—the future that we need to create for effective ministry to students.

Youth Ministry 3.0
A Manifesto of Where We've Been, Where We Are, and Where We Need to Go

Mark Oestreicher
Retail $12.99
978-0-310-66866-4

Visit www.youthspecialties.com
or your local bookstore.